THE VISITOR'S GUIDE TO
THE YORKSHIRE DALES,
TEESDALE & WEARDALE

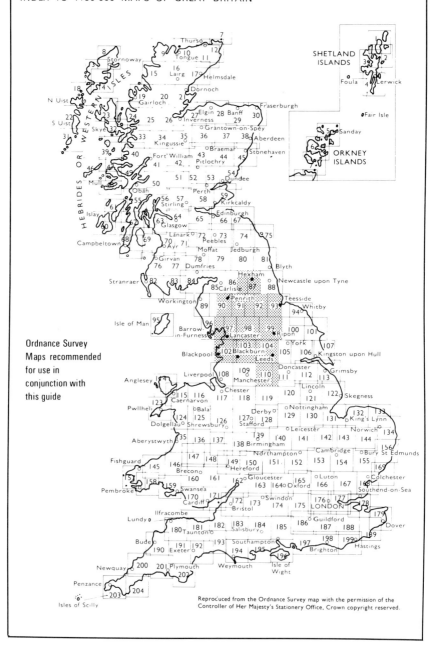

INDEX TO 1:50 000 MAPS OF GREAT BRITAIN

SHETLAND ISLANDS

ORKNEY ISLANDS

Ordnance Survey
Maps recommended
for use in
conjunction with
this guide

Reproduced from the Ordnance Survey map with the permission of the
Controller of Her Majesty's Stationery Office, Crown copyright reserved.

The Visitor's Guide To

THE YORKSHIRE DALES, TEESDALE & WEARDALE

Brian Spencer

MOORLAND PUBLISHING

HUNTER
PUBLISHING INC.

British Library Cataloguing in
Publication Data

Spencer, Brian
    The visitor's guide to the Yorkshire
Dales, Teesdale & Weardale. — 2nd
ed.
    1. Yorkshire Dales National Park
(England) — Guide-books
    2. North Yorkshire — Description
and travel — Guide-books
    I. Title
914.28′404858   DA670.Y6

Photographs on pages 72 and 75 are by A.
Mays; pages 50 and 56 are by G.N. Wright.
The remaining black-and-white photographs
were taken by the author.
    Colour illustrations have been supplied by:
J.A. Robey (Arkengarthdale, Wharfedale); B.
Spencer (River South Tyne); the remainder
are by R. Scholes.

ISBN 0 86190 155 X (hardback)
ISBN 0 86190 154 1 (paperback)

Published in the USA by
Hunter Publishing Inc,
300 Raritan Center Parkway,
CN94, Edison, NJ 08818

ISBN 0 935161 49 X (paperback)

Printed in Great Britain by
Butler and Tanner Ltd,
Frome, Somerset.

Contents

Introduction

When Moorland Publishing invited me to write this guide they originally specified that it should essentially be devoted to the Yorkshire Dales. My first reaction was to ask: what and where are the Yorkshire Dales? Certainly there is an area of land which fits this title within the boundary of the Yorkshire Dales National Park, but surely the dales do not stop just at the boundary of the National Park, for they continue north and south. I do not accept these rigid boundaries as we are all of the same race and speak the same language. Of course customs and dialects change and long may they remain, but I believe that the dales occupy most of the Pennine chain and for that reason I decided to expand my original brief to include the northern dales.

A few years ago I did a photographic essay of the Pennine Way and to get the shots I wanted, I spent months wandering up and down the length of the Pennines, not just along the 'Way' but also through the side dales and valleys. One of the things which came out of this exercise was a realisation that it is impossible to put any form of boundary on the Pennines before the Newcastle/Carlisle gap. This then confirms my decision and I am glad that the publisher has agreed.

I was born almost in Lancashire, and certainly my upbringing owed allegiance to the Red rather than the White Rose; however my wife and I spent the first eight years of married life across the moors from Haworth and this is when my real affection for the dales began. We spent every free weekend and holiday exploring the delights of the southern dales and gradually became aware that here is a part of our country which never ceases to provide new sights and experiences if one is prepared to look around off the beaten track.

During my early courtship with the fells and dales, one April I took an American friend over my favourite hill, Penyghent. We were lucky to find the purple saxifrage in full bloom on the hills near Penyghent Pinnacle and then on the journey back to Horton we stopped to look at Hunt Pot. My friend gazed into its depths and then told me that if this had been America there would have been a fence round the hole, with a guide permanently in residence to stop people falling into it and also to give lectures on its mysteries. This horrified me, as we have too much control as it is and God forbid that we ever reach the stage where we are controlled and organised like that. I only hope he was exaggerating, but I would like to think that his statement made me determined to write my guide in such a way as to encourage readers to go out on voyages of exploration and not to be led everywhere by the hand.

The thing which came out clearly while preparing this guide, is the friendliness of the people who live in the dales. As you wander through the dales I hope you will enjoy meeting them as much as I did.

Brian Spencer

Note on the Walks Described

The walks suggested in this book are not intended to be a field-by-field guide, but recommendations for the best routes. Many have been chosen so that they avoid the popular and crowded areas, while many are more interesting or give better views than the better known routes. Walkers must be equipped according to the severity of the terrain: strolling or woodland walks requires only stout shoes and weather protection. High level moorland walks need proper boots and clothing, map and compass and the ability to use them correctly.

The method used in describing the walks assumes that the walker will carry with him a map of 1:50,000 scale (about 1¼in to the mile) or better still 1:25,000 (about 2½in to the mile). These latter are available as Ordnance Survey Outdoor Leisure Maps, giving cover to much of the Pennine area between the Peak District and the 'Three Peaks' (Whernside, Ingleborough and Penyghent.) It is, of course, important that the walker is familiar with the use of maps, especially the use of the Grid Reference — this is a skill which can be developed in the winter evenings, by the fireside!

The Ordnance survey maps which cover the area of this book are:
1:50,000 Landranger Series, sheets 87, 90, 91, 92, 97, 98, 99, 102, 103, 104, 110.
1:25,000 Outdoor Leisure Series,
The Three Peaks
Malham and Upper Wharfedale
South Pennines

The walks described have been graded so that a suitable route may be chosen at a glance. Both distance and walking time are included, but the latter is often of more relevance.

H	High level route for fine weather conditions
M	Medium level route
L	Low level route, often recommended when the weather is poor on higher ground
o	Least interest
oo	
ooo	
oooo	Most interest
*	Well signposted
**	Easy to follow with the aid of a map
***	Requires careful map reading
****	Recommended for experienced hill walkers only

Rights-of-Way

A number of walks described in this book are across open moors or limestone pavement. Although in some instances official rights-of-way do not exist, all the routes have been walked for many years by countless people without hindrance, are still regularly used and feature in most local guidebooks. It is hoped that in the near future formal agreements can be arranged for free access.

KEY FOR MAPS

�	MUSEUM/ART GALLERY/CENTRE
⌒	SHOWCAVE
⊿	ARCHAEOLOGICAL SITE
⊞	BUILDING/ COUNTRY PARK GARDENS
Π	CASTLES
✻	OTHER PLACE OF INTEREST
∩	ABBEYS

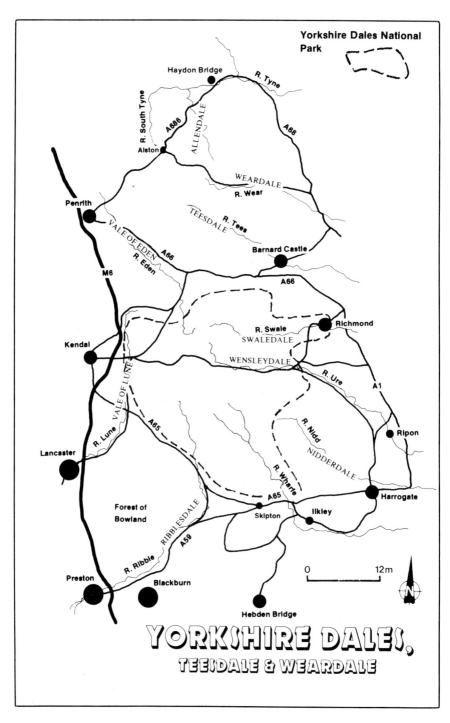

Yorkshire Dales National Park

YORKSHIRE DALES,
TEESDALE & WEARDALE

1 The Yorkshire Dales

This book is about part of that highland mass which makes up the backbone of England known as the Pennines. The Pennines are made up of a loosely linked series of hills reaching to almost true mountain height but keeping mostly to broad ranging moors with an average height well below 2,000ft. Although the Pennines have only a few distinctive summits above this height it must be clearly stated that their character is closely linked to mountain masses when it comes to weather, especially in winter. The different character of the dales and valleys carved into the moors and separated by high-level roads is still apparent even with the standardisation of farming methods. This character has to a large extent, withstood the population changes brought about by economic demands or the easier transport of the twentieth century.

The Pennine Dales are very often thought of as being solely within the confines of the Yorkshire Dales National Park boundary, but their character extends much further north and south of what are mostly the limestone dales. The Pennines can be regarded as starting north of Derby, and include the Peak District, whose high gritstone moors continue north of its official boundary into the mass of bleak uplands between the M62 and Calderdale. North of Calderdale the character of the hills changes slightly and soon the industrial valleys give way to broader and more pastoral dales. These in turn narrow and

deepen as limestone begins to dominate in the Craven district north of Skipton.

Across Stainmore, beyond the A66, the broad fastness of the Teesdale and South Tyne uplands differ in appearance from their southerly cousins, but still have an essential Pennine character. This is different from say, the Lake District or the Cheviot, even the Peak District is different. For these reasons therefore the dales we are about to explore are those valleys draining the high ground north of Calderdale and on as far as the South Tyne Valley.

The word Pennine originated in a forgery produced by Charles Bertram, a professor of English at Copenhagen University, in 1747. He claimed to have discovered a fourteenth-century manuscript 'De Statu Britannica', a treatise on Roman Britain, which said that the country, Britannia Maxima, was divided into two equal parts by a chain of hills known as the Alps Penina (Penine Alps). No doubt the name was a fanciful link with the Apennine Hills of Italy. Until 1822 no one bothered to group the individual heights under a single heading and it was two geologists, Conybeare and Phillips, who decided on the name when writing about the rocks of Northern England, and ever since, the word Pennine it has been the backbone of England anything else would be unthinkable.

The hills and dales of the Pennines have not always been what we see today — change, though slow, is the only constant thing about them. The time scale over which the Pennines evolved spans 300 million years, but even by that scale they are mere nothings compared with the 4,000 million and more years that the earth has taken to develop. When ancient mountain ranges were being worn down to become the muddy floor of a tropical sea, volcanoes were active to the north, which formed the basis of the Cheviot and other rounded hills of Lowland Scotland and the Borders. Life in the sea was prolific with countless millions of tiny organisms and shell fish living and dying in a warm environment. Gradually their bodies built up layer upon layer into limestone, often to a depth of hundreds of feet, sometimes around coral reefs, but usually on the flat muddy remains of the ancient, or Silurian mountains. A huge continent far to the north was drained by a mighty river emptying into this shallow sea, and gradually a delta appeared which slowly filled the sea with a fine mud which eventually packed down to become shale, and covered the limestone remains of the earlier sea creatures. This covering action was not at a constant rate and allowed mud flats to develop with lagoons in between. More limestone accumulated in these lagoons before it, too, was covered by more mud and silt. As the delta moved further south, larger particles of sand or grit were left behind by the river and these in their turn compacted to make Millstone Grit. As an indication of the quantities involved, it has been estimated that the Millstone Grit layers of the Pennines once covered an area of more than 25,000 square miles and are the results of the destruction of a mountain range 6,000 miles long, 20 miles broad at the base and two miles high. As the

delta developed, swamps appeared which supported tree-like plants, and when they in turn died their remains were compacted in the peaty swamp to become coal.

During the time that these rocks were being formed, the earth underwent periods of activity. From deep down mineral solutions were forced upwards through weak points in the rock structure and on nearing the surface began to cool, to give veins of lead ore, fluorspar and other minerals. In addition, a huge sheet of molten rock thrust its way over a large area of limestone in the northern Pennines. This intrusion, now known as the Great Whin Sill, extended from the Farne Islands to Cross Fell and is responsible for the dramatic crags on which Hadrian built the Roman Wall. In the Pennines it appears as such important features as the waterfalls of High Force and Cauldron Snout, and also in the columnar crags around High Cup Nick.

During all this activity there was no sign of any of the dales as we know them. In fact the folds and cracks which eventually became the dales are the result of earth movements which also made the Alps and the Himalayas. These movements were active between seventy and one million years ago. After this lifting up, rivers flowed down the folds and gradually deepened them into valleys. Later the various Ice Ages covered all, except the highest summits of the Pennines, with a huge sheet of ice which ground down into the valleys, widening and deepening them. As the ice melted with the return of warmer times, vast amounts of water gave further shape to the dales, or disappeared beneath the softer limestone to form cave systems and potholes. Sometimes glacial action wore away the top layers to expose older rocks as is the case at Malham Tarn where a lake nestles incongruously amongst limestone. The rock beneath the tarn is slate and completely impervious to water. Rock and clay debris from retreating glaciers were left behind to further alter the shape of the landscape and this is usually seen in the form of elongated low humpy hillocks such as are found below Gargrave in Craven and in Upper Ribblesdale. Other earth movements resulted in such unique features as are found in the Malham area where the layers of rock beneath the Cove actually started life on the same level as the summit of Fountains Fell some four hundred feet higher. These later movements, or faults, are again a major feature of the modern landscape, such as the South-Craven Fault which is responsible for the line of limestone cliffs east of the A65 Skipton to Ingleton road.

After the last major upheaval had finally settled, and the glaciers gave their polish to the contours of the dales, the pattern we know today was left behind. This pattern of twisted and bent folds generally radiates from a line which starts with Cross Fell and continues south east beyond Great Shunner Fell. Hills make valleys or as is the case of the Pennines, hill ranges make the dales. The Ribble begins on the flanks of Ingleborough, and to the north, the Lune drains south from the Howgills. The River Eden's source is within half a mile of that of the Ure but Cross Fell and the Lakeland Fells force it into a northwards course while the Ure flows east, down Wensleydale. The far northern dales of Tees, Wear and South Tyne originate in a geological complex east of Cross Fell known as the Alston Block.

Further south the Askrigg Block generates the main rivers of the dales, Swale, Ure, Wharfe and their tributaries.

The Ribble and Eden drain almost unpolluted into the Irish Sea and are excellent sporting rivers for the angler who can often find salmon as well as trout. The northern valleys of Teesdale, the Allendales, Weardale and the Derwent valley have beautiful rivers for most of their length but are disfigured by industry along their lower reaches. The main rivers of Yorkshire's dales, the Swale, Ure, Wharfe, Nidd and Aire all drain into the Ouse, thence into the Humber. With the exception of the Aire they have relatively clean waters all the way to the sea. The Aire, despite its lovely birth, becomes in its lower reaches a disgraceful record of man's industrial callousness. Although pollution has been reduced there is much still to be done before the sparkling beauty of Malhamdale's Aire continues along the whole of its course.

When a warmer climate returned after the last Ice Age, mosses gradually colonised the bare rocks, in turn providing soil for small alpine-type plants, which later gave way to a forest which once covered the whole of the non-limestone part of the Pennines. The trees on the high parts were dwarf birch and mountain ash, while lower down pines gave way to oak and beech woods, with the limestone region supporting grasses and alpine flowers.

Man came late on the scene and, some would say, with disastrous results. The first men were purely hunters able to exploit the prolific life abounding on the Pennines, their first permanent homes were in caves such as Victoria Cave above Settle where the remains of reindeer and grizzly bear have been found. The abundance of these animals normally found now in sub-arctic tundra regions, suggests that the weather was not unlike that of today. As later man became more sophisticated he built settlements and grew crops. With this came the need for a calendar to regulate his year, and ensure that crop planting coincided with the correct season. This problem seems to have been overcome by the erection of stones aligned with sun or star rise at specific times of the year. Later refinements lead to complex stone circles and possibly the enigmatic stone carvings on Ilkley Moor.

About this time man settled the sparsely wooded highlands of the limestone area, but with the pressures of a growing population the first of the forest clearances took place, a development which continued well into monastic times and which has only been reversed recently through reafforestation. As man progressed, a primitive consumer society grew up with trade in metals, furs and pottery. Trade was particularly strong between Ireland and Europe and the natural easy route through the Pennines, known as the Aire Gap, was on the direct way between the two areas of population. Craven and the area around Skipton became a busy centre very early on in this island's history.

The Pennine's greatest mineral asset, lead ore, exploited by the Romans, continued in medieval days, but the main expansion of lead mining occurred during the eighteenth and nineteenth centuries when improved water supply and roofing meant a greater need for this versatile material.

The Romans left many relics in the remote dales, and in fact they would appear to have lived in fear of the wild Brigantean tribes who inhabited the area. They built a town on the site of modern Ilkley and quite probably the southern part of the dales was settled by peaceful tribes. Further north things were much different and the east-west road across Stainmore (a route which is still followed by the modern A66) was very heavily defended. One of the native leaders who did not accept Roman domination was Venutius, who built a fort on the summit of Ingleborough as his headquarters. By AD74 Venutius was defeated and many of his followers ended their days as slave labour working for Rome in the lead mines of Greenhow near Pateley Bridge.

With the withdrawal of the Roman legions, the dales, as with the rest of Britain, entered a period known as the Dark Ages. In Mallerstang, Pendragon Castle has links with the Arthurian legend. It was during this time that missionaries from Ireland began to spread Christianity through the dales. Their usual method was to link the new beliefs into the old pagan ways in the hope of gradually overcoming the old with the new. So strong, however, were some of these old faiths, that even though their origins are lost in the mists of time, there are still traces around to this day, customs like the Easter Pace Egg ceremonies at Heptonstall in Calderdale.

From the sixth century onwards successive waves of people came from the European mainland to northern Britain. Angles, Vikings and Norsemen all subsequently became settlers, bringing their own farming methods, their own cultures, their own language. Place-names such as the Angle 'ley' meaning a forest clearing; for example Otley, Ilkley and Wensley.

The Danes' settlements are identified with their 'by' ending, following the name of the owner, like Thoralby, Melmerby, etc. If there was a church nearby the name became Kirkby as in Kirkby Lonsdale. Norsemen left the names of features, which have gone into our vocabulary as 'skeli' or 'scale' for outlying farms such as Winterscales and Summerscales, but their major impact on our vocabulary was to leave us words of natural features such as fell, gill, beck, mere, moss, heath and ling. Two of the most visible links with early time which can still be seen around the dales villages are cultivation terraces known as lynchets, and the narrow strip field systems which resulted from the necessity to plough long furrows using the heavy cumbersome ox-drawn ploughs of the time. Good examples of these can be seen around Grassington and Burnsall, in Wharfedale; in Wensleydale near Aysgarth, and in Coverdale.

No sooner had the British King Harold killed his Norse enemy, and namesake, at Stamford Bridge in 1066 than he too was killed at Hastings, which left the country open to the cruel Norman tyranny under Duke William. Norman relics are the many solid castles which guard the dales and command the major routes. Much of the Pennines was preserved as royal hunting forest and terrible punishments were enacted on anyone caught poaching the royal game. Many ancient offices were set up to control the forest which though having no power today, are still remembered and their customs preserved.

During the Norman influence the monastic orders grew in size and importance and the abbeys became some of the major landowners in the dales. It was during this time that the final clearances took place and forest gave way to hill pasture to feed the growing flocks of sheep. Living standards were improving all the time and monastic fortunes were made on wool. Even the fourteenth-century ravages of the Black Death which wiped out a tremendous part of the population in Europe had only a momentary effect on this trade, and the monasteries continued to prosper. As the size of the abbeys and cathedrals increased so did the demand for lead for their roofs and so the monastic orders who were never slow to realise an asset, developed those lands where lead could be found. This in turn meant more felling of forest to provide fuel for the smelters, and an alternative fuel was sought. Coal found on Fountains Fell and around Tan Hill was mined in shallow bell-shaped pits.

In the sixteenth century Henry VIII broke the power of the monasteries by taking away their lands, treasure, and eventually destroying the magnificent abbeys. The result of this action remains to be seen in the now mellow ruins made tranquil by time and weather.

From about 1300 to 1600 the dales were vulnerable to marauding bands of Scots who came south, well into Craven, on their cattle raids. These raids were mostly carried out by small bands of men, marauding into the more remote corners of the dales stealing and generally making a nuisance of themselves; the small skirmishes which developed have gone down into folk lore as though they were huge battles. A fray in Weardale for instance, honoured by a folk song of thirty-seven verses, was fought between only a few dozen men. The pele tower, a square defensive farmhouse, was developed about this time and allowed animals and family to share the same roof in safety until the danger passed. Nappa Hall, in Wensleydale, and Mortham Tower near Barnard Castle, are two fine examples.

As times became more civilised and the population started to move towards the towns and cities a more peaceful Scot began to arrive on the scene. Increasing demands for fresh meat by town dwellers made good markets for Scottish beef cattle and gradually a trade developed with animals being brought on the hoof from the Highlands.

The dales suffered badly in the King's cause during the Civil War. Many of the castles which were still homes of the nobles and lesser gentry, were besieged (sometimes for months on end) by troops led by Cromwell in support of Parliament. Skipton Castle, which suffered badly, was owned by the Clifford family, and Lady Anne Clifford in the quieter and more peaceful times after the restoration of the monarchy set about rebuilding it and other family properties.

A prominent feature of the Dales' landscape is the enormous number of stone walls. Hundreds of miles of them snake up fellsides, pattern valleys, and form small fields near old villages. Almost all of them are at least a hundred years old, most date from the period of Parliamentary enclosures between about 1770 and 1840, and some — mainly those forming irregular boundaries to tiny crofts behind houses in old villages — are of sixteenth century date or even earlier.

With the steady growth of industry throughout the north, the move to the towns and cities was ever constant, but the effect of the Industrial Revolution was to give it new impetus.

Subsequent decline of lead-mining caused movement away from the dales. The demand for dairy produce and wool has given stability to dales farming, and mechanisation and increased mobility have brought marked changes to life in the dales. Few villages have declined; some, closer to centres of industry, have actually grown as commuters make their homes in them. Some provide holiday homes, and most rely to some extent on tourism.

Dales architecture has been slow to change, and most dales' buildings date from between the mid-seventeenth to late nineteenth centuries. Some houses and barns have outside stairs. A few fortified towers are incorporated into later farmhouses. Each dale has its proud castle and ruined abbey usually in a riverside setting. Stone continues to be the one constant building material used in every type of building, and strict planning control ensures that new domestic building is in harmony with the old. Modern farm structures, however, are outside such strict control, and some are particularly aggressive in the landscape.

Transport has always played a major part in the dales scene, from ancient trackways to Roman roads connecting regional headquarters like York and Lancaster. Later came the cattle drovers whose roads can still be traced, often as walled green lanes. Countryfolk often travelled miles on foot or horseback from one dale to another to reach a nearby market. Likewise, the bulk produce of wool, carried on the backs of ponies on its outward journey to the weaver, would meet returning pack trains laden with finished goods for sale, or salt to preserve winter meat. All these ancient methods of transport created their own roads and where they cross the remoter parts of the dales or the high moors, they can still be easily followed, often for miles, from one linking motor road to another.

The road system began to improve with the Turnpike Acts around the middle of the eighteenth century, good quality roads were built by private enterprise. These roads were a vast improvement on the old trackways and helped speed up movement between the centres of population by allowing wheeled vehicles to travel easily on their superior surfaces. The turnpike in turn became the foundations of today's motor road system.

Between 1770 and 1790 the Pennines were crossed by canal between Leeds and Liverpool but its effectiveness was soon to be challenged by steam locomotion. In the second half of the last century railways spread to the remoter parts of the dales to reach some of the lead mining areas and quarries. Most of these lines are now abandoned but the most scenic of them all, between Settle and Carlisle, is still open.

Industry came early to the Pennines with the discovery and exploitation of lead and other metallic ores, and production came to a peak in the late eighteenth and early nineteenth centuries. Up until then most mining was carried out by small teams of men who would only work proven veins, but gradually the concessions were bought up by various companies, some with a strong Quaker foundation, and the pattern was set of paternalistic employment with good standards of housing, and an education for the miners and their families. Lead mining areas, which declined through the competition from cheaper imports, have found a new lease of life with the demand for fluorspar used as a flux in steel making. Once a waste product it is now a much sought-after material, particularly in the Weardale area.

Agriculture is the oldest industry, and the beginnings of planned farming came with the growth of the monasteries. The monks developed new and improved strains of sheep yielding more and better wool, and specialised breeds appeared in the dales. Of late the rearing of sheep as a cash crop has diminished with a reduced demand for home bred wool and the distinctive local breeds have become more mingled with general purpose crossbreeds. Domestic industry such as the manufacture of knitted stockings, once so important has vanished and likewise few farms now make any cheese for sale.

Quarrying stone for building thrived locally at the end of last century. Today, increased demand for limestone for road-stone and cement has become concentrated in parts of Craven and Weardale.Mountainous regions are providers of water, but only the part not on limestone is suitable for this. The major catchment areas are Bowland, Nidderdale, Baldersdale and Upper Teesdale, where reservoirs introduce a new element into the Pennine scene.

Today's demands on the dales are more intense than ever before. Easier transport means that more people go into the hills either as day or holiday visitors, and a significant number commute from those villages within reasonable distance of the major towns. The most attractive areas are unfortunately the most popular and heavily used. Malham can become very crowded during a holiday period as can Ingleton, Settle, Hawes and

Aysgarth. On busy weekends these are places to avoid by those seeking solitude. The quieter areas are around the Howgills north of Sedbergh and in the Northern Dales, and in the lonely little valleys which no motor road reaches.

With the passing of the National Parks Act of 1949, consideration was given to the setting up of a National Park in the Yorkshire Dales; by 1953 the boundaries had been decided and the area of 680 sq miles enclosed by them was designated as a National Park.

The park is controlled by a committee of the North Yorkshire County Council, which is augmented by members of the three district councils whose areas encroach into the park: Craven, Richmondshire and South Lakeland; by a representative of Cumbria County Council and — perhaps most importantly — by eight members (one third of the total committee) appointed by the Secretary of State for the Enviroment to represent the *national* interest in this national asset.

In accordance with the 1949 Act, the Committee is charged with two prime objectives: to 'preserve and enhance the natural beauty. . . of the area' and 'to promote opportunities for (suitable) outdoor recreation'. At the same time, the committee has a declared policy of carrying out its main responsibilities with the interest of the local population in mind. Obviously, within these guidelines there is often conflict; in such cases decisions are generally weighted in the favour of good conservation practice.

The National Park Authority has responsibility for planning and development control in the park, but its main contact with visitors is through its 'field services': the Warden Service (responsible for footpath maintenance, patrol and guidance at sites popular with visitors, public and educational liason and liason with local farmers); the Information Service (there are six National Park Centres in the Dales, manned by staff capable and ready to answer the tremendous variety of questions which visitors ask); and on the guided walks which are organised throughout the summer season.

The walker is well catered for in the Dales. There is a wide variety of accommodation, from campsites to hotels, from Youth Hostels to bunkhouse barns, from caravan sites to warm and friendly village inns. It is calculated that there are about a thousand miles of public footpath and bridleway in the National Park alone; the Pennine Way traverses the Dales on its route from Edale to Kirk Yetholm, while the Dales Way links Leeds with the Lake District.

In the following chapters, the routes of walks have been carefully selected and graded. None are too difficult for anyone who is reasonably fit. The choice of footwear and clothing will depend on the individual, but novice walkers would do well to read *Rugged Country Rules* (available from National Park Centres). Watch the weather, and leave a note of your route before setting out.

2 Ribblesdale

Although born in Yorkshire, the Ribble is, in its maturity very much a Lancastrian river. It has long been a favourite outdoor area for people from the nearby industrial towns of North Lancashire and as a result farmhouse and coaching inns of earlier times have developed a tradition providing food of excellent quality. Their close proximity to each other in the Ribble and Hodder valleys ensures a spirit of competition and consequent high standards.

Lancashire's Ribble is a favourite

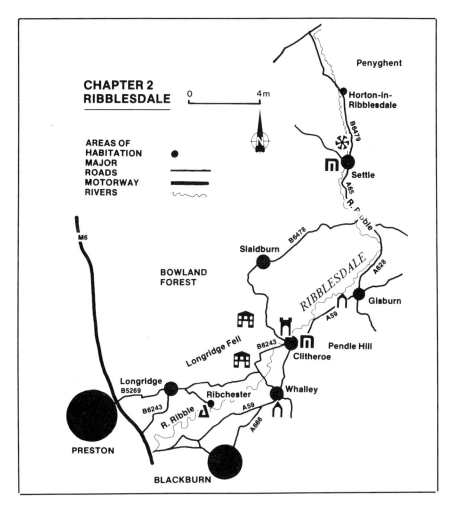

amongst picnickers, motorists and fishermen. The Ribble downstream of Ribchester is noted for its sea trout and the occasional salmon which are caught on their return journey to spawning grounds upstream. Apart from one or two popular places like Edisford Bridge near Clitheroe or at Ribchester, nowhere does it get over-crowded, even on busy bank holidays.

As this guide is essentially dealing with dales which are mostly in Yorkshire, it is only logical that we should move upstream describing Ribblesdale from the sea to its source at Ribblehead, where the Ribble is well and truly a Yorkshire river.

Working up river from midstream Preston, the first place of note is the Roman fort of *Bremetennacum* on the edge of Ribchester, a quiet town of interesting old weavers' cottages. A grass bank outlines the outer walls of the fort and only the ruined walls of the granary are left of what would have been an important centre at the crossroads of east-west and north-south routes. The site was well chosen to command a safe river crossing over the Ribble, although now a large part of the southern defences have been washed away by changes in the river's course. The late thirteenth-century church of St Wilfred now occupies most of the fort.

Nearby Longridge Fell is a favourite haunt of devotees of hang gliding and if you want to watch this graceful sport there is an easy walk following any of the paths across the fell above Hurst Green. These will give you views of Bowland to the north and the whole length of Ribblesdale to the south and east. A suitable starting point is along the path from Brook Bottom (SD 676404) north-west towards Weed Acre and then turn east

along the road to Walkerfold and south by the path across the fell back to Brook Bottom.

Stonyhurst College above Hurst Green is a Catholic college run by the Jesuits.It was founded in 1593 as a school for English Catholics, but due to repressive laws against catholics during the reign of Queen Elizabeth I, it was set up at St Omers in the Low Countries. After a chequered history and many moves, in 1794 following the French Revolution, the college made its way to Stonyhurst, a Tudor country house with close links with an important local family, the Shireburns. Since then the building and college have prospered and it is now one of England's leading Catholic schools. The oldest part of Stonyhurst dates from 1594, but there have been additions in every century, especially the nineteenth, right up to the present day. Oliver Cromwell stayed here, and slept fully clothed on a table during the Civil War fighting in Lancashire. The college is situated at the end of a sweep of a magnificent avenue and is open to the public by arrangement with the Assistant Bursar, to whom application should be made by letter.

The river which flows round the base of Longridge Fell is the Hodder. Sleepy unspoilt villages and prosperous farms are spaced along its length. This is the boundary between Lancashire and Yorkshire and the villages have that indefinable Yorkshire character; it is another world from the industrial towns not so very far away south of the Ribble.

Almost hidden down a side street of Whalley are the ruins of Whalley Abbey which make a quiet setting for the Blackburn Diocesan Conference centre and Retreat House. The abbey was built between 1330 and 1380 and at the Dissolution of the monasteries in the 1530s it passed in 1553 into the Assheton family, who converted the Abbots Lodgings into a manor house. It is this section which remains as the Conference Centre with the ruined part of the abbey set off by banked flower gardens.

Chipping has some industry, chairs are made here, but at Dunsop Bridge, Newton and Slaidburn, the atmosphere is almost feudal. Visit the Hark to Bounty Inn in Slaidburn and in an upstairs room you will be shown a courtroom where a primitive justice was handed out until more enlightened times. The inn is named after a famous hound from a local pack which had a distinctive cry. St Andrew's Church down the road is mostly Jacobean and has some interesting family pews. The red sandstone Jacobean building of Browsholme Hall, home of the Parker family, ancient guardians of the 'Park' of Bowland, is open to the public.

Bowland's rolling moors are a jealously guarded grouse preserve, and fell-walking is restricted to a few tracks. One to the south west of the Trough of Bowland follows Langden Brook (SD 632512) and then climbs steeply up and over Holme House Fell south west to Bleasdale Tower and the road to Oakenclough. Unless you can arrange transport for the return journey this tough walk must be repeated to get back to a car parked above Dunsop Bridge. Near Bleasdale is the site of a wooden henge, (SD 577460) now marked by concrete pillars, the remains of the stumps and full details of the layout can be seen in Preston Museum.

A round tour by foot from Dunsop follows the Trough road as far as Rams Clough (SD 628522) and then by Trough House and path across Whin Fell to Brennand House. From

H
7m
3½h
oo
***

M
7½m
4h
oo
***

Slaidburn Church

19

Places to Visit Around Clitheroe

Ribchester
On the B6245, $4\frac{1}{2}$ miles north of Blackburn. Pleasant riverside village with interesting weavers' cottages in the street leading to the remains of the Roman fort of Bremetennacum. Outline of the fort can still be seen; the granary has been excavated as part of the perimeter fort wall now washed away by changes in the river bank.

Whalley Abbey
On the A59, 4 miles south of Clitheroe. Built between 1330 and 1440. After the Dissolution of the Monasteries, in 1553 the property passed into the hands of the Assheton family where it remained until 1923, when it was acquired by Blackburn Diocese. Now a conference centre and a retreat house. Tranquil ruins and attractive gardens, craft centre/gift shop.

Clitheroe Castle Museum
Displays on the theme of life in the nineteenth century.

Stonyhurst College
Hurst Green, 4 miles from Clitheroe on B6243. Public school founded by the Jesuits in 1593. The house, dating from 1337, retains many interesting architectural features. Open to visitors by appointment.

Browsholme Hall
Near Bashall Eaves, 6 miles north west of Clitheroe. Home of the Parker family, keepers of the Forest of Bowland since 1507. House has been added to and altered by subsequent generations. Fine oak panelling and a collection of armour and relics of the Forest of Bowland.

Museum of Steam
On the A682, 2 miles south of Gisburn. Small collection of steam-driven vehicles. Traction engines, showman's engines, fairground organ, all steamed during the summer. Open at all reasonable times. Free.

L
$8\frac{1}{2}$m
4h
ooo
***

here a track round the side of Middle Knoll leads into Whitendale and a right turn down the farm road back to Dunsop Bridge.

A lower-level riverside walk starts in the village of Slaidburn and follows the Newton road for about a quarter mile beyond the church and then turns right on the path above Dunnow Syke as far as the junction of the path between Pain Hill and Clerk Laithe. Turn left here and down into Newton. Walk through the village and across the river to follow the south bank down stream as far as the road at Gibbs Farm. Turn left along the lane which climbs slowly up from here to the Waddington road. Turn right and follow the road for half a mile, then

left by a track leading down past Smelfthwaites. Beyond the farm turn left again on a path down to Easington. A path leads over a slight rise and then across the Hodder and back to Slaidburn.

From Slaidburn the road goes south across Waddington Fell past the Walloper Well (SD 717483) where you can make a wish, towards Clitheroe and back into Lancashire. Waddow Hall on the Clitheroe road outside Waddington is owned by the Girl Guides Association.

The market town of Clitheroe manages to retain its agricultural character despite the closeness of nearby limestone quarries. Its castle has what is reputed to be the smallest keep in

Bowland

the north and the hole in its south wall is supposed to have been made by Cromwell's cannons during the civil war. It was built by Roger de Poitou, son of Roger de Montgomery, one of William the Conqueror's commanders at the Battle of Hastings. There is a local legend of a battle when King Stephen of England fought the Scots under William Duncan outside the town in 1138.

The footpath between Low Moor and Brungerley Bridge is an ideal strolling place on a summer's evening. This walk can be included in a visit to Clitheroe Castle and makes for a most pleasant evening.

The whaleback mass of Pendle Hill commands the view south east from Clitheroe. This is witch country where stories abound, some true and others of folk origin. The villages of Newchurch and Barley have made the most of the dreadful wrath meted out to the poor unfortunates in less enlightened times and local curio shops specialise in witchlore. Old ponds

attached to now ruined mills from a time when cotton was king in the Pendle area are well stocked with fish, mostly coarse but often brown trout which have been introduced by local angling clubs. Most of the waters are owned by local clubs and permits to fish must be obtained beforehand.

Pendle Hill in a storm can readily conjure thoughts of a witches' Sabbath, but on a fine day the steep pull up from Barley by way of Ing Ends to the summit is worth the effort. A long walk can be made by returning across Pendle Moor and Spence Moor to Newchurch or alternatively carry on to the Nick of Pendle and back to Barley by way of a series of tracks which contour around the southern flank of Pendle. This way goes by Craggs, Ratten Clough to join the Newchurch road at Sabden Fold. A left turn along the road and down to Barley completes the hard but enjoyable route. A stranger to this area will soon realise why the inhabitants of the nearby cotton towns take such a proprietorial interest in Pendle. All the little nooks and crannies with their

H
9m
5h
oooo
****

21

remains of old industry cry out to be explored. The small information centre in the car park at Barley will help a first-time visitor find out more. The high road round the 'Big End' of Pendle leads to Lancashire's prettiest village, Downham, and then back into Ribblesdale.

Farther up the Ribble, the next stop is Sawley with its scanty remains of a larger Cistercian abbey. North west from Sawley a path follows the west side of the river, then by Tosside Beck to Bolton-by-Bowland. Return by walking east up the Gisburn road to Cow House Hill and then a field path south-east to Fooden. Turn right here above the Ribble to Bolton Hall, and across Tosside Beck in Bolton village to rejoin the path to Sawley.

Lush pastures between Clitheroe and Settle produce some of the region's finest cattle and sheep. This is the southern edge of the Craven district of Yorkshire, with Gisburn its western gateway and market village on the A59. To its north Hellifield provided homes for railway workers on the lines which have their junction a little

L
7m
3½h
ooo

way beyond the village. The famous Settle-Carlisle line is the most dramatic section of a main railway route from Yorkshire to Scotland, although not so busy as formerly, but at least trains still run! The other line from Hellifield runs through the Ribble valley by way of Clitheroe to Preston. The river is to the west of Hellifield and wanders through flat meadows which at times flood after heavy storms higher up the valley.

If you want to explore these pastures then there is a route from Paythorne, two miles north of Gisburn on the A682. It goes by field path to Pie Cross Plantation (SD 814532) then on to Higher Aigden, northwards to Moss Side Farm, then east to the village of Halton West. Two miles of path south across Paythorne Moor completes the tour back to the starting point.

Settle is a popular stopping place both for people moving into the higher dales or beyond and for those who appreciate Settle for its own worth. There has been a market here since a charter was granted in 1249 and the old town hall denotes its

L
5½
3h
oo

Downham Village and Pendle Hill

Places to Visit Around Settle

Museum of North Craven Life
Victoria Street, Settle.
Displays show how man has made use of the countryside around Settle since prehistoric times.

Pig Yard Museum Castle Hill, Settle.
Located in a converted eighteenth-century warehouse. Exhibits of outstanding archaeological items from caves in the Dales, especially Victoria Cave. Also remains of hippopotamus, bison, rhinoceros, hyena and other Ice Age mammals. Open by appointment only.

Shambles Settle.
Remnants of 'Old Settle', an interesting cluster of old shops to one side of the market square.

Victoria Caves
2 miles east of Settle on Attermire Scar. Scene of excavations which proved that the caves were lived in from Neolithic times to the Roman occupation. See p24 for walk.

Stainforth Bridge and Force
Below Stainforth on B6479
An elegant arched packhorse bridge on the highway between Lancaster and York. Owned by the National Trust. Stainforth Force, down-stream a hundred yards, rushes over limestone edges into a deep, black pool and can be reached by a footpath from the bridge.

Ebbing and Flowing Well
Buck Haw Brow. on A65 1 mile north west of Settle.
By the roadside, about half way up the hill. When working the well empties itself without warning and then just as mysteriously refills.

Market Square. Prominent on the other side is the Naked Man café which was once an inn. The name and sign are said to be devised by the innkeeper as a protest against the excessive fashions of his time. Settle is busy and yet at the same time a refreshing town sheltered from the coldest winds by Langcliffe Scar to the east, so that it can be quite the sun trap its gardens proclaim.

Coaching inns dating from the seventeenth century indicate the early importance of Settle as a link in the chain of communications. It was a handy resting place before the steep climb up Buck Haw Brow on the Keighley to Kendal turnpike road. The railway superceded this more romantic method of travel and the line which goes north from here to Carlisle ranks as one of the most courageous feats of engineering. When it was built in the 1870s the army of navvies who passed across the sleepy acres of Ribblesdale must have appeared to the locals like the hordes of Gengis Khan.

Two small but excellent museums in Settle tell the story of life in bygone days in this part of mid-Craven. These are the Pig Yard Museum on Castle Hill and the Museum of North Craven Life in Victoria Street. The Pig Yard Museum contains the remains of many animals discovered locally, some extinct, but others now found only in Equatorial Africa, which is an indication that the climate of Britain was once much warmer than now. These relics, the left overs of the meals of our ancient forebears, were found in Victoria Cave on Langcliffe Scar. Other exhibits of sophisticated utensils and weapons dating from the Iron Age have led archaeologists to suggest that the cave was used as a refuge

importance as an administrative centre for the area. The unusual building known as the Shambles dominates the

when the Romans came up into Craven in their search for lead.

Every March there is a well supported drama festival in Settle, with guest celebrities taking part in what has become a most ambitious series of events.

Langcliffe and Attermire Scars are the visible surface indications of the Mid Craven Fault, a massive shift in the strata of the earth's crust. This fault is in evidence all the way from Malham to Settle. From Settle to Ingleton it continues as the South Craven Fault, which forms an impressive natural boundary of the limestone uplands, most conspicuous at Giggleswick Scar.

M
5m
2½h
oooo
**

An easy five mile walk from Settle follows a path beneath Langcliffe Scar where there is an opportunity to explore Attermire and Victoria Caves. This walk leaves the town centre by way of Banks Lane (beyond the Shambles and Constitution Hill). Where a clump of trees appears on the right, turn right and climb upwards to Attermire Scar. Turn left and follow the wall to a series of caves, the largest of which is Victoria Cave. On to a junction of four walls with a stile to help you climb them. Turn left on a cart track to the Malham to Langcliffe road by Clay Pits Plantation where a sharp left turn away from the road leads back down to Settle.

Across the river from Settle, but bypassed by the busy A65 is Giggleswick which retains old and gentle charm. The Norsemen settled here and in the twelfth century St Alkelda founded what is now Giggleswick's parish church. It is perhaps the famous public school with its green domed chapel, which brings most acclaim to this place. The school was founded by James Carr as a charity school in 1507.

Hull Pot

24

M
·m
·h
·oo
*

The South Craven Fault continues as Giggleswick Scar where the A65 climbs steeply up Buck Haw Brow. About two thirds of the way up is the Ebbing & Flowing Well. On the rare occasions that the well functions, it rapidly drains, and then after a pause refills itself. This is due to a unique double chambered cave somewhere behind the well which causes a sudden syphoning effect inside the hole and temporarily cuts off the flow of water.

Giggleswick Scar can be explored from a path which climbs up through Lords Wood to the cairn built by boys from Giggleswick School. The path climbs gently beneath the scar to meet the A65 at the top of Buck Haw Brow.

The National Park sign at Langcliffe marks entry into the Yorkshire Dales National Park. Northwards up Ribblesdale is true limestone country where the Settle to Carlisle railway competes with the B6479 for the available space in the valley bottom. A couple of miles above the quiet back lane between Giggleswick and Little Stainforth is the enigmatic feature known as the Celtic Wall. This is an ancient stone wall almost 70ft in length, 5ft high and 5ft at its base. The purpose of this wall is in doubt, but archaeologists believe it is over 2,000 years old. To reach the Celtic Wall take the field path which climbs north west from Stackhouse into what is locally known as Happy Valley. Turn left at the top gate in Happy Valley and climb the escarpment to the Celtic Wall (SD 800676). Follow the escarpment beyond the wall and turn right on the Feizor to Little Stainforth path and eventually back to Stackhouse.

·
·⁄₂m
·
·oo

Stainforth was settled before the Norman Conquest and its prettiest features are Catrigg Force high up above the village, and the pack horse bridge which once carried the old drove road from Lancaster to York. A river and fellside walk takes in both of these features and starts at Stainforth by climbing up Goat Scar Lane. At the top of the lane is a gate and Catrigg Force is below on the left. At the top turn right on a farm track to Upper and Lower Winskill farms. On around the brim of an old quarry and into the lane to Langcliffe. Turn right, follow the B6479 to the point where it crosses the railway and turn left along a lane and down to the Ribble. Cross the river and follow its west bank to Stainforth Bridge and back to the village. Where the Ribble flows through a narrow gorge above Stainforth it really shows its power, especially in spate after heavy rain or melting snow.

Further up the dale beyond Stainforth and Helwith Bridge comes the first glimpse of Yorkshire's famous mountain trio. To the right is Penyghent, left is Ingleborough, and beyond but not seen for another few miles is Whernside, Yorkshire's highest point, 2,419ft above sea level. These are the 'Three Peaks' one of the hardest expeditions open to the fellwalker and that toughest of all sports — cyclocross. While not wanting to scorn the efforts and energy of fell racers, there is however, a certain distaste in the thought of the fells becoming places of competition against anything but oneself. The Three Peaks Walk is certainly a fine expedition for the really hardy fellwalker. To cross the 25 miles of very rough ground and climb a total of 5,000ft within the hours of daylight will certainly create a sense of achievement. Only those who are fit and have a previous knowledge of the terrain should attempt this walk. Limestone country

L
4m
2h
oooo
*

is full of snags, from small outcrops to sheer-sided pot holes, all lying in wait for the unwary walker. The walk was started in 1887 by two school-masters from Giggleswick who walked over Ingleborough with the intention of having tea at Chapel le Dale. Whernside tempted them on and once there, Penyghent completed the challenge. The route has been run in around four hours or cyclocrossed in less then three, but usually needs all the hours of summer daylight.

There are few rules controlling the Three Peaks Walk apart from the really important one about doing it in daylight, and the need to complete the circuit in one go. Most people start at the Three Peaks Café in Horton in Ribblesdale and walk the route anti-clockwise. The café proprietor has installed a factory clocking-in machine and participants are expected to clock 'in' and 'out'. The proprietor expects anyone who drops out for any reason to let him know as the fell rescue services are automatically called out at the end of the day against any in-complete cards. This also applies to anyone who completes the walk, but fails to clock back in again. So if you do the walk, please comply with this very simple but effective scheme. The rescue service people do not take too kindly to being called out on a wild goose chase!

The route of the three Peaks Walks is very well described in Wainwright's *Walks in Limestone Country* and it is fairly easy to follow with the aid of the Ordnance Survey map. However the following notes should act as a rough guide.

Starting from Horton take the Settle road as far as the bridge beyond the parish church. Turn left over the bridge and past the school to Bracken-bottom Farm, where a clearly sign-posted path leads up the hillside to join the Pennine Way path, then steeply up the outcropping crags to the summit of the first peak, Peny-ghent. Cross the summit to a break in the western cliff. Go downhill for about quarter of a mile and fork right in a north westerly direction (the main path goes back to Horton via Scar Lane). Walk downhill and aim to the right of the distinct shape of Hull Pot. **Note that if you cannot see Hull Pot then it is either too dark or misty and you should call the whole expedition off and live to try again.** Continue along a faint track still north west through, or better still, around the bog of Black Dub Moss and in about a half a mile turn right on to the bridle way from Horton to Langstrothdale. This section again coincides with the Pennine Way, but leaves it at Old Ing Farm. Take the farm lane left and about halfway to the neighbouring High Birkwith Farm turn right and follow a drystone wall to God's Bridge, a natural bridge of limestone, and Netherlodge Farm. The farm road leads down and across the infant Ribble to the B6479 beyond Ingman Lodge. Turn right along the road and aim towards the Ribblehead viaduct. To combat erosion on the steep south-eastern slope of Whernside, a new route has been created; keeping to the *east* side of the railway as far as Force Gill, it follows the Craven Old Road towards the easier contours of the northern slope. A signposted path takes a gentle curve away from the Old Road to reach the summit of Whernside. After a rest near the summit cairn go left from the South-Western ridge and aim steeply downhill to Bruntscar Farm and its road to Chapel le Dale and Hill Inn. Unless the Hill Inn is too irresistible, walk north up the Ingleton-Ribblehead road to a stile on the right of the road and start to climb again. This section of the walk across the north-west slopes of Ingleborough is dotted with caves and pot holes and is worthy of the lengthier exploration which we are saving until a later chapter. For the final lap of the Three Peaks walk it is necessary to walk back along the track from the top of Ingleborough to the lowest point of the col in the direction of Simon Fell. Turn right in a south easterly direction across marshy ground, past Sulber Pot and across three walls to a wall above Beecroft Quarry. Follow the wall towards the south and at a shooting butt turn left over a stile and follow a cairned path around the quarry to Beecroft Hall and eventually over the railway and back to Horton remembering to clock back in at the café.

After all that strenuous exercise perhaps a short gentle digression is called for, and what better than to comment on the wild life and history of the area? The most common sound on the high fells is made by the curlew. Its haunting call is evocative of the windswept rough grass moors which it finds ideal for its nesting sites. Ravens and crows inhabit the high crags and lower down, the fells are the haunt of lapwings whose call gives rise to its other name 'pee-wit'. Pied wagtails live in open country near water, but their larger relative the grey will rarely be found away from streams and ponds. Of all the birds of north Ribblesdale the warbling song of the skylark as it climbs high into the sky brings home the joy of summer. Plant life abounds. On the high peaty tops are bilberry and cloudberry. Purple saxifrage festoons the lower crags, then mountain pansy and bird's eye primrose with the insectivorous plants the sundew and butterwort in boggy places. Ferns such as hart's tongue

Horton-in-Ribblesdale Church with Penyghent behind

enjoy the damp recesses of fissures in the limestone pavements. Cotton grass and the purple moor grass together with white mat-grass cover the lower slopes between the high tops and limestone outcrops.

It was the sweet grass of limestone country which for centuries provided grazing for sheep bred for their fleeces. Monastic wealth came from wool and vast areas of the dales were once owned and farmed by the Cistercians of Fountains and other abbeys. The whole of upper Ribblesdale was one vast sheepwalk divided amongst the abbeys of Fountains, Furness and Sawley. Ingman Lodge near Ribblehead was once a grange for Furness abbey. Change affects most things in life and improvements in stock-breeding brought about breeds suited to their environment. The Swaledale and its variant the Dalesbred are particularly favoured now. The Swaledale has a grey nose on a black face and the Dalesbred has white patches on its face. Other breeds are the Rough Fell and Wensleydale, but the Dalesbred is the most common in this area.

The village of Horton-in-Ribbledale is an ideal centre for exploring the woods and caves of Upper Ribblesdale. Unfortunately you must try to ignore the quarries along Moughton fellside to the west. The one above Helwith Bridge quarries Silurian Slate which was once used for paving slabs, the sides of rainwater tanks and even tombstones, but now the stone is only wanted for road building. Beecroft is a limestone quarry with the attendant smoke which regretfully appears necessary with lime and cement production. Despite this nearby industry, Horton is a hospitable place, an obvious stopping place for people walking the Pennine Way, exploring the maze of cave formations around the village, or just enjoying the delight of the open spaces around. The church dates from Norman times and is built of local materials from the slabs on the floor to the lead on its roof. Look at its Norman doorway and stained glass windows, especially the west with the ancient fragment showing the mitred head of Thomas à Becket. Do not worry if you get the feeling that the place is leaning because it really is! All the pillars lean to the south and have done so for generations, so there does not seem much danger of the church falling on your head yet! While a number of east windows in dales' churches have a definite slant, nowhere does the whole church interior lean like it does at Horton.

Penyghent is the obvious mecca for most walkers starting from Horton. The majority take the way up and down Horton Scar Lane, but a more enjoyable route is the one which follows the Three Peaks Walk route through Brackenbottom farm from Horton to Penyghent, then down to Hull Pot before joining the Horton Scar Lane back to the village.

There is another and shorter walk using Horton Scar Lane and linking up with another short stretch of the Pennine Way. This way follows Scar Lane out of Horton as far as Hull Pot before turning left to follow the Three Peaks track across Black Dub Moss to the Horton to Langstroth green road. Turn left at this point and past Sell Gill cave system and back to Horton. Although the Three Peaks path across Black Dub Moss is not a right-of-way hundreds of walkers follow it annually, and it is hoped that free access can be negotiated.

H
$5\frac{1}{2}$m
3h
ooo
**

M
4m
$2\frac{1}{2}$h
oo
***

28

Hidden in tiny ravines amongst this expanse of rolling moorland are the charming survivors of ancient woodlands left over from a time when our climate was much milder than it is today. Ling Gill, four miles north of Horton is a National Nature Reserve, easily reached by a short walk from the road end near High Birkwith farm (watch where you leave it if you come by car, do not block the field gates). Follow the green lane to Old Ing farm and join the Pennine Way which, in about one mile passes above Ling Gill ravine. At Ling Gill bridge, which was built in the sixteenth century, a tablet refers to its repair in 1765 'at the charge of the whole of West Riding'. Cross over the stream at this point and leave the Pennine Way and aim for a barn at the junction of three walls. Turn left and walk above Ling Gill to Nether Lodge farm where another left turn crosses a couple of fields and God's Bridge back to High Birkwith.

One of the delightful features of the dales and one of which the last three walks make full use, are the green roads. These are ancient roads, often dating from monastic times, which may be traced for miles across open country. They were used originally to connect outlying sheep areas with the parent monasteries and later were used as drove roads when cattle and sheep were walked south from as far away as the Scottish Highlands to the industrial market of the south. The roads, often unwalled, always follow the easiest gradients and best grazing to feed driven animals, or the pack horses which carried the commerce of developing industry, before the advent of steam. One such road is the track

Penyghent Pinnacle

from Feizor which crosses the Ribble below Stainforth and then climbs out towards Malham before continuing as Mastiles Lane into Wharfedale. Around Horton, Moor Head, Long Lane, Horton Scar Lane, Birkwith Moor Lane and the Sell Gill Lane are all ancient green roads.

From Stainforth to Ribblehead the vast depth of limestone is riddled with water-worn features in the form of pot holes and caves. This is the realm of the specialist for whom the excitement and danger of exploring the unknown is ever present. There are no show caves in Upper Ribblesdale, but for those skilled in the arts of cave exploration another world opens up beneath your feet. Even now there are long distance routes being discovered in linked cave systems which only a few years ago were just theories. Nowadays access to the larger cave systems is controlled by a central body, so membership of a recognised club is essential, but most welcome beginners to the sport.

Of all the pot holes in the area, Alum Pot is perhaps the most picturesque, sheltered amongst trees with Alum Pot Beck falling with a frightening 200ft plunge into its depths. Another stream enters beneath the surface from Long Churn to the north west. Water entering Alum Pot does not drain directly into the Ribble but passes beneath it to feed Turn Dub on its far bank. Turn Dub is the tiny pond between the river and the larger Newhouses Tarn above the word River on the OS map. Alum Pot can be reached by an easy path from Selside and Northcote Farm and this walk can be extended to take in the rest of the cave system connected to Alum Pot. A small charge is made at Northcote Farm for use of a private path.

1m
½h
000◖
*

At Ribblehead where the magnificent sweep of the railway viaduct spans the dark moorland, an interesting introduction to the varieties of caves and limestone crags can be made by wandering along the cart track from the Ribblehead Inn. Just before the tracks go under the viaduct turn right across open moorlands and aim for the limestone pavement above Runscar Scar, here you should pass at least ten assorted caves before crossing the B6255 to follow Thorns Gill

M
4½r
2h
000◖
**

Places to Visit Around Ribblehead

Ribblehead Viaduct
6 miles north west of Ingleton
Opened in 1876 it carries the Settle to Carlisle railway across some of the wildest upland country in England.

Horton Scar Lane
Horton in Ribblesdale
A typical example of a 'green road' and ancient trackway still in regular use by local farmers and walkers. Connects Horton in Ribblesdale with Halton Gill in Littondale.

Cave Systems around Ribbleshead
An easy walk passing many interesting caves and potholes. For details see pages 28, 30.

Penyghent
2½ miles north east of Horton in Ribblesdale.
An easy climb in fine weather. For details see pages 26, 28.

Horton Church
A delightful dales' church built of locally-quarried slate and limestone. Lead on its roof was probably mined locally.

Ribblehead Viaduct

downstream and enjoy its wealth of semi-alpine flowers. There is no right-of-way across the limestone pavement, but it is a well used route. Turn right at a footbridge and aim upwards towards a barn where a left incline will lead you towards the road which is either followed or left in favour of a parallel route on the moor with softer walking.

It is not often that man-made objects can improve the face of nature, but one of the few exceptions is surely the graceful span of twenty-four arches which make up the Ribblehead Viaduct. Built in five years by hundreds of navvies who lived in a primitive camp at Batty Green, the viaduct is an important link on the Settle and Carlisle Railway. Tales of disease and horrific accidents abound in the making of the viaduct and Blea Moor Tunnel just to its north. The tunnel took four years to complete and the work was done by candle light (the bill for candles alone was £50 per month). No one knows how many men died in making the line for they mostly lie in unmarked graves at Chapel-le-Dale on the Ingleton road. Their true memorial is in the Settle-Carlisle line which runs through some of Britain's grandest scenery.

3 The Lune Valley

Some of the most attractive yet least-known countryside of Northern England lies between the Yorkshire Dales and the Lake District. The most popular area is around Ingleton and yet not far away is an area of equally rewarding country with quiet villages and secluded side valleys, which runs through Kirkby Lonsdale and Sedbergh to the Howgill Fells in the north. This is almost unknown territory.

The Lune valley separates the Dales from the Lakes, yet its river owes

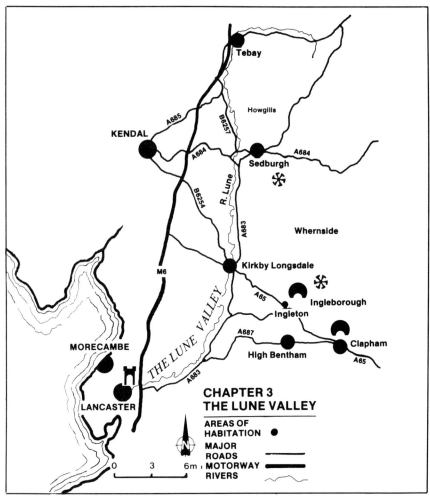

**CHAPTER 3
THE LUNE VALLEY**

AREAS OF
HABITATION   ●
MAJOR
ROADS
MOTORWAY
RIVERS

0   3   6m

Devil's Bridge,
Kirkby Lonsdale

Flinter Gill, Dent

The Howgills

Beckfoot, Lune Valley

allegiance to neither and has a character of its own. Only around its south-eastern tributaries do we find limestone, the result of the North Craven Fault. Northwards shales and gritstones predominate all the way up to and including the Howgills. It is these fells which feature strongly in the birth of the Lune. The river starts its life as a number of becks flowing northwards from the north-east flanks of the Howgills. It then flows west and south to be joined by the Rawthey below Sedbergh. It bounds three sides of the Howgills before flowing south west into Morecambe Bay.

Looking through the arches of the Ribblehead Viaduct from Runscar towards the B6255 Hawes-Ingleton road the view on the left is of Ingleborough and to the right the vast bulk of Whernside rears menacingly above Blea Moor. The high country on either side of the road between Ribblehead and Chapel le Dale is flat, but suddenly the road begins to switch back and the most distinctive features to the landscape are the tiered limestone cliffs of Raven Scar to the left beneath Ingleborough and Twistleton Scar buttressing the south west slopes of Whernside on the right.

Above Raven Scar the limestone pavement is worth visiting. Leave the road by a gate opposite the lane to Dale House Farm and ascend the hill by an easy track which climbs through the three tiers of Raven Scar to a sheepfold. A little further on by a wall on the left and surrounded by a wire fence is Meregill Hole. This is one of the major cave systems of the Ingleton area and descends 520ft in the direction of Ingleborough. Turn right from the hole, cross more than a mile of pavement to White Scars and join the Ingleborough path down by Fell Lane

into Ingleton. A word of warning here to anyone attempting this walk in unsuitable footwear — limestone is slippery when wet and it is easy to sprain an ankle. Also note that this is not an official right-of-way, but this route is one used regularly.

Soil build up on limestone is very sparse and the level strata allow acidic rain water to erode deep fissures and crevices into the flat pavements. Beneath Raven Scar and close by the road is White Scar Cave which is open to the public. Good illumination enhances the beauties of its varied rock formation and stalactites.

Ingleton is a busy and popular tourist centre, which originated as a farming community, but grew into an industrial village working local limestone, slate and coal. Water from the River Doe powered cotton and woollen mills. Tourism started in 1849 when the railway arrived and crossed the deep ravine of the Greta by a viaduct which dominates the town. Man has known Ingleton a long time, the B6255 follows part of the Roman road linking the fort of Bainbridge in Wensleydale with the regional headquarters town of Lancaster. Today tourists bring a good income to the town whether they stay for only a quick cup of tea, or overnight at one of the many bed and breakfast houses, the youth hostel or the excellent hotels and pubs. Ingleton has a very good outdoor heated swimming pool and fine community centre.

Before moving northwards to the source of the Lune we must explore its southern tributary, the Wenning which drains Ingleborough. The old road from Ingleton to Clapham more or less follows the line of the North Craven Fault where the limestone sits firmly on top of slate. Limestone allows water to sink through but it cannot penetrate slate and so must reappear.

H
8m
4h
oooo
***

A walk which takes in the geology of the mountain starts in Ingleton. Follow the B6255 until just before Storrs Hall where a right turn leads off from the road up Fell Lane past Storrs Cave and gradually ascends the south-west slope of Ingleborough on what is for part of its length a delightful, soft grassy track. On top of Ingleborough turn right and follow the ridge to the south, then bear slightly left towards Fell Beck and Gaping Gill where a gradually improving path drops down through Trow Gill to Clapham Beck. Pass Ingleborough Cave and enter Clapdale Woods with its Reginald Farrer Nature Trail. These are privately owned woodlands of the Ingleborough Estate who make a small charge at the cottage above the lake. Clapham is just beyond and refreshments are usually easy to find before catching the bus back to Ingleton.

The distinctively tiered bulk of Ingleborough gives clues to the eye of the trained geologist to whom each layer indicates a separate feature with different objectives unique in itself. To the observant walker who relates contours and names on a map the first will be Storrs Cave, just beyond the start of the path to Fell Lane which is an old mine working on the site of a cave entrance. Quaking Pot marked on the OS map is actually only the middle one of three pot holes close together on the 1,450ft contour. The bones of Ingleborough make themselves evident on the line of ascent. Ingleton stands on slate and immediately above the town there is a 600ft layer of limestone and this gives the easiest walking of the climb with gentle gradients and soft grass under-

foot. Above Quaking Pot a 1,000ft band of shales and sandstone which have eroded more easily show up with the steepening angle of the path. Later harder and less eroded shales give way to a final escarpment of millstone grit 100ft thick. The summit of Ingleborough is a fascinating place to the archaeologist, but even an untrained eye will notice the regularly shaped piles of stones scattered about on the plateau which marks the summit. The first pile seen on the left at the top of the last and steepest part of the climb are the remains of a tower built in 1830 by a local millowner. Only the curved stones of its base remain to indicate its size. Beyond are two modern features, the triangulation point and a shelter seat made in the cross shape to give protection from all wind directions. A view indicator has been sited at the centre of the shelter walls giving the names of all the major landmarks of the superb panorama visible on a clear day.

Towards the eastern edge of the plateau are the remains or six or so prehistoric hut circles. Beyond is a ruined wall, said to be Roman, but attributed by others to an ancient tribe known as the Venutians who were beseiged here by the Romans. Who built the huts and for what purpose on the waterless but easily defended point, is not known. If the wall is Roman, then quite possibly Ingleborough was used as a signal station, making full use of the fact that it can be seen over a great distance from Cumbria and well down into Lancashire. Beacon fires have blazed in celebration of great occasions in the past.

South from the top and away down the shales of Little Ingleborough the return to limestone is marked dra-

Gaping Gill

matically by the most famous of all pot holes — Gaping Gill, 360ft deep with a waterfall dropping into a chamber high enough to contain York Minster. The true grandeur is all underground, for at ground level there is just a crater where Fell Beck disappears. The clue to its dangers is only given by the flimsy sheep fence around its perimeter. At spring and August bank holiday periods caving groups divert the stream and erect a chair and winch, which all may use. No charge is made for the descent, but the return journey must be paid for! Anyone contemplating the trip must be prepared to get wet and a bit muddy, but otherwise for the really adventurous this can be quite an exhilarating trip.

Cave explorers — including divers — have attempted to open up routes between Gaping Gill and Ingleborough Cave in both directions; surveys show that they have reached the line of Trow Gill from both ends, but as yet a vital few yards has eluded all attempts to make the through journey. Ingleborough Cave is open to the public and is one of the oldest show caves in the Pennines. It was made accessible when a wall of limestone

which had held back an underground lake was demolished by use of explosives in 1837.

Downstream from the cave the path enters an area of peaceful woodland; this is Clapdale Wood, part of the Ingleborough Estate. Although privately owned, the public are allowed here, hence the need to pay a small toll at the end. Little of the woodland is natural, having been improved by successive plantings. The stone grotto and lake are additional man-made features.

Ingleborough Hall and its estate, together with much of the village of Clapham, was owned by the Farrer family of whom Reginald Farrer (1880-1920) was probably the most well known. Farrer was the father of alpine flower collecting and became a great authority on the subject. He travelled widely in mountainous regions of the Far East in search of the flowers and shrubs, some of which can be seen today in Clapdale Woods. The story is told of Farrer returning from expeditions in the Himalayas and refusing to greet his family until he had seen his specimen plants safely potted up and tended. The Reginald Farrer Trail within the woods as far as

Trow Gill is named in his memory. A brochure describing the trail is usually available from the National Park Centre in Clapham.

Two miles east of Clapham, and just off the busy A65, the village of Austwick was settled first by the Norsemen. It had a market once, but lost it to Clapham. This is a quiet, gentle village with many attractive old houses, the hall belonging once to the Ingilbys, an important local family.

Above Austwick during the last Ice Age a glacier which filled nearby Crummack Dale, deposited many large boulders of Silurian rock about half a mile away on the underlying limestone. Subsequent weathering of the surrounding softer limestone has left some of these boulders perched on top of small white pedestals. These are the Norber Boulders, or erratics, to give them their correct geological term. The boulders are above Nappa Scars and can be reached by a path starting at a gate close by the crossing of Thwaite Lane and Crummack Lane. The gate is on the Clapham side of the cross roads. This path continues

M
4m
2h
oooo
***

The Way to Ingleborough

up on to Norber Hill passing the perched boulders of the way. The source of the boulders can be seen on the right three fields away towards Crummack Farm.

A longer walk which starts and finishes in Clapham follows Thwaite Lane from the village. After about a mile climb over the wall on the left by using a stile which is indicated by a footpath sign. Climb up slightly to the right across the field and follow a wall all the way up to Nappa Scars and the Norber Boulders. Continue along the Scar as far as Norber Brow and cross the road. Turn right to follow a field path into Austwick. Bear right in the village centre. At the far end of the village a signpost on the right indicates the field path back to Clapham.

South and west of the A65 marl, a clay made from limestone during the Ice Age, gives excellent pasture on either side of the River Wenning which flows through the small towns of High and Low Bentham to the Lune. The fells to the south are part of the Forest of Bowland and the roads lead to Slaidburn and the Ribble. Several of the short field paths west of Lower Bentham on the south side of

M
8m
4h
oooo
***

36

Places to Visit Around Clapham

Norber Boulders
1 mile north east of Clapham
Erratic Silurian slate boulders left by retreating ice on the 12-15in high pedestals of limestone. For description of walk see pages 36, 37

Clapham Village
On A65, 6 miles north west of Settle
A charming village on the Leeds-Kendal turnpike, now designated as a Conservation Area. Yorkshire Dales National Park Information Centre in centre of village.

Clapdale Woods
$\frac{1}{2}$ mile north of Clapham
Landscaped woods laid out by the Farrer family of Ingleborough Hall. Many shrubs and plants of Himalayan origin planted by Reginald Farrer (1880-1920), an internationally famous authority on alpine plants. Nature trail within the woods.

Ingleborough Cave
$1\frac{1}{2}$ miles north of Clapham
Show cave, easily accessible by footpath through Clapdale woods.

Gaping Gill
3 miles north west of Clapham
Impressive pot-hole with a vertical drop of 340ft. Local caving clubs erect a winch-borne chair on Spring and August Bank Holidays.

the river, can easily be linked up to make a pleasant summer's afternoon walk down to Wennington and back.

The village of Wray is at the junction of the rivers Hindburn and Roeburn and was almost destroyed when a cloudburst high up in Roeburndale caused the river to burst its banks. Wray was once a place of thriving industry with basket weaving and clog making. Silk top hats were also made here at one time. On a rise between the Hindburn and the by now deepening Lune, stands Hornby and its castle. Built soon after the Norman Conquest the castle was owned by generations of Neville and Stanley families until 1643, when it was captured by Colonel Ralph Assheton, Commander of Parliamentary troops in North Lancashire. For some unknown reason the castle was not destroyed as was normal in such cases and it remained a home for many years. The present building was erected by Edmund Sharpe who was mayor of Lancaster in 1848.

In our journey around the tributaries of the Lune we must return to Ingleton to find one of the most attractive walks in Britain. This is the round of Ingleton's waterfalls. The Craven Fault dips to the south here and has created a series of limestone steps over which two rivers cascade in sparkling beauty. This is a very popular $4\frac{1}{2}$ mile walk and one where only the unscrupulous avoid the small toll.

Take the B6255 opposite Ingleton bus station and drop down to cross both the Twiss and Doe, turn right along a signposted lane to the car park and the little kiosk where you will be asked to pay a small entry fee. Walk on towards the trees of Swilla Glen where the valley narrows to a short ravine. The path follows the west bank of the Twiss for about a mile before crossing over for a short distance below the twin Pecca Falls. Here the route crosses back and gradually leaves the woodlands behind, climbing steeply past a refreshment hut to the highest of Ingleton's waterfalls. Thornton Force falls 46ft over an amphi-theatre of limestone to the older slate rocks beneath, and is a famous geological location. Above

L
$4\frac{1}{2}$m
2h
oooo
*

2-3m
$\frac{1}{2}$h
ooo
***

Thornton Force

the Force the track loops upwards and then above Raven Ray swings to the right across the River Twiss for the last time and enters Twistleton Lane then a right turn to Twistleton Hall, where refreshments are available. On a clear day the view to the south of the Bowland Fells from Twistleton Lane is sufficient excuse for rest. Beyond Twistleton Hall a signposted field path aims for Beezleys Farm across a lane which is the main road between Ingleton and Chapel le Dale. A short distance below the farm the River Doe which has been flowing gently down the valley suddenly cascades over a series of narrow rocky outcrops known as Beezley Falls and continues noisily down through Baxengill and Yew Tree Gorges to drop over Snow Falls. The path keeps closely to the river before crossing it at the bottom of the steep Twistleton Glen, then continues upward through the trees and comes out into the ruins of old quarry workings below Skirwith Beck. Ingleton is a short distance away.

Whernside can be climbed from Ingleton on the long 11½ mile route which starts above Twistleton Hall off the Chapel le Dale Lane. Follow the Waterfalls walk for a few yards away from the farm in the direction of the river, but swing away to the right

H
11½
6-7
oo
***

and aim for the left side (facing) of Twistleton Scar. The next section is across open country and not on a right-of-way, but normally access is allowed. Gradually by following the boundary wall, the path climbs the broad south west ridge of Whernside to West Fell and steeply above Combe Scar to the highest point of Yorkshire. To return follow the same route to the bottom of the steepest section of the summit ridge and at a cairn below Low Pike turn left to follow the Three Peaks route for a little way down to Bruntscar Farm. Right here along a short lane with a wood on the right. At the end of the lane cross a narrow field to Ellerbeck Farm. Leave the farm lane at the ford by the gate below the farm and turn right to climb easily up Rigg Side to rejoin the ascent path beneath a huge stone built into the boundary wall. A mile and a half of down hill will bring you back to Twistleton Hall.

The Craven Faults and surface limestone gradually disappear to the north of Ingleton. Barbon Fell is to the east of Casterton where the tell-tale signs on the map still show pot holes and caves. This is still the territory of the speleologist or cave explorer, but the walker can enjoy Kingsdale and Leck Dale and the intervening fells.

On the north side of Kingsdale the level moorland above Keld Head Scar offers a whole series of interesting stones, pot holes and caverns. One, Yordas Cave, was once a showplace, now abandoned and hidden from sight inside a small wood (SD 705791). If you take a good torch and do not do anything foolhardy once inside it is possible to explore this cave. The entrance still retains its steps and the best feature of the cave is the Chapter House, a circular chamber with an attractive slender waterfall. The cave floods after heavy rain, but is not dangerous, only very muddy afterwards. The best way to get to Yordas Cave and all the other limestone features above Keld Head Scar is either to walk up from Ingleton or leave a car tidily parked on the Dent-Ingleton road somewhere in the vicinity of the Twistleton Lane. Look for an old limekiln and aim for the OS column above the Tow Scar. A hundred yards or so to the right is the Cheese Press Stone — an unusually smooth faced limestone boulder. Swing round to the right a little way above the OS column and join the delightful grassy track known as Turbary Road. This was originally made to ease the way for horse drawn sledges which brought peat down from Turbary Pasture. The 'road' follows an easy terrace and makes for pleasant walking while viewing a whole complex series of pot holes on either hand. While Turbary Road climbs upwards on to the moor, aim for the trees surrounding Yordas Cave and rejoin the Dent road where a right turn will take you back to the starting point.

H
6m
3h
oooo
***

Round the other side of the hill from Turbary is Gragareth. An unusual name for these parts and sounding like something out of a novel by Sir Walter Scott. The name should act as a draw, but apart from three fine cairns on its western shoulder and an excellent view from the top, there is little to excite the interest on the way up. On a fine clear day the climb from Ireby on the road to Leck Fell House, past the Three Men of Gragareth on to the summit is a short walk and worth the effort.

The next tributary dale is that of

8m
3½h
oo
**

Leck Beck which in its upper reaches forms the boundary between Lancashire and Cumbria. Leck Beck drains the great sweep of fells starting at Ease Gill and culminating at Great Coum. The last of the limestone before it finally disappears underground, shows up dramatically in the lower reaches of Ease Gill. Its rock formations and sinks can be explored in a short but interesting walk from Bullpot Farm at the end of a three mile macadamed road from Casterton. Follow a field path to the south beyond the farm, which is now a caving club hut; beyond is Bull Pot of the Witches. Pass some old lime kilns to Hellot Scales Barn and enter the Gorge of Easegill Kirk where Leck Beck flows out on the surface. Turn left up the normally dry valley and after a mile of very rough walking on boulders a complex system of pot holes and caves is reached. It will be necessary to retrace your steps for about half a mile at this point to find an easy way out of the valley on the right (it should be fairly obvious, but it is not serious if you turn either too soon or too late). Make for Lancaster Hole whose entrance is covered by a manhole, and back to Bullpot Farm. One word of warning in conclusion, Ease Gill disappears beneath the ground through a system of sinks and in a period of heavy rain they cannot take all the hugh volume of water flooding down from the cirque of fells from Gragareth to Great Coum and Craghill. Once the sinks fill they overflow and the normally dry river bed becomes a torrent.

Casterton Fell can be climbed in a short walk from the road, either by the lane which starts at SD 641793 on the OS map or more or less directly from the other end of the lane close by Gale

M
3½m
2h
ooo
***

H
2m
1h
oo
***

Garth Farm. Neither route actually crosses the summit, but it is reached by a short deviation about the 1,300ft contour line.

The village of Casterton is an ancient place where standing stones and circles abound. Its development as a wool centre in the Middle Ages led to the building of a walk mill where wool cloth was felted, or fulled, by foot in the soft waters of a side stream to the Lune. The Brontë sisters attended a Clergy Daughter's School here and before that King Henry VIII stayed nearby at Kirfitt Hall when he was courting Katherine Parr of Kendal Castle. The house is supposed to be haunted by the headless Anne Boleyn ever searching for her fickle king and husband.

Kirkby Lonsdale is on the west bank of the Lune from Casterton. The A65 crosses on a modern bridge, but upstream is an earlier structure known as the Devil's Bridge — a graceful triple arched span of unknown age, but certainly recorded in 1275 when funds were found for its repair. The story which connects it to the Devil is that an old lady wishing to cross the Lune found the ford deep under water. The Devil appeared and offered to build a bridge on condition that the first living creature to cross it would belong to him. She thwarted him by throwing a bun across the bridge and a small dog chased it to become the first across.

Kirkby Lonsdale is 'Cherkaby Lownesdale' in the Domesday book (Kirkby means church town). Its church is certainly of Norman origin. A charter granted in 1272 to hold fairs and markets was disputed, but a Thursday market has been held regularly since 1335. During the 1715 rising, Jacobite soldiers assembled

Places to Visit Around Ingleton

Ingleton
Off A65, 17 miles from M6 junction 34 South western gateway to the Yorkshire Dales. Popular tourist village with several inns and restaurants. Heated open-air swimming pool nearby.

Glens and Waterfalls of Ingleton
A delightful walk through wooded glens follows the River Twiss upstream and Doe downstream, passing waterfalls of breathtaking beauty. See pages 27, 31, 33 for the description of this walk.

Ingleborough
3½ miles east of Ingleton
A straightforward climb in fine weather. Interesting archaeological remains on the summit. Fine view point. See pages 25, 26, 27, 34 for the description of this walk.

White Scar Caves
1¾ miles east of Ingleton on B6255. Show cave accessible by road. Car parking.

round the market cross. An afternoon of strolling round Kirkby Lonsdale and the nearby river towards Devil's Bridge will be rewarding. At one time the artificial water course along Market Street worked seven waterwheels driving industries which ranged from bone-crushing to snuff-making.

Steep sided Barbondale is softened in its lower reaches, close to its name village, by woodland which surrounds turreted Barbon Manor. Even though Barbon is an old place and by-passed by the modern A683 from Sedbergh, which here follows more or less the line of a Roman road, commercial traffic in pre-railway times avoided the village, keeping about a mile away to the west. At High Beckford the neat symmetrical lines of a pack horse bridge spans Barbon Beck. Pleasant waterside paths radiate from Barbon up and down its beck and through surrounding fields, but a greater challenge is the circuit of Middleton Fell. This is also a walk for botanists who will find many rare sub-alpine plants and orchids growing on the open moorland.

The Middleton Fell walk starts from Barbon centre by the bridge and follows the beck for about a quarter mile upstream then a left turn through Barbon Manor Park makes for Eskholme Farm. Turn right at the farm and climb steeply up Eskholme Pike, across Thorn Moor to Castle Knott. On to Calf Top (the highest point of the walk at 1,999ft), to Green Maws then swing round across Long Bank where an improving track leads eventually to Fellside Farm and the main road. The Ribble Bus company operate a service along this road and careful planning will help the tired walker to use it for a return to base. The alternatives are to arrange for a co-operative driver to pick you up, or walk back along the field path which visits practically all the farms to the east of the A683 to Barbon. The fell takes its name from a group of farms rather than any particular village. Middleton Hall was never fortified and as a result suffered severe damage during the Civil War when Cromwell's troops broke through the west wall of the courtyard.

Below Sedbergh the two northerly and major side rivers join before being in their turn joined by the Lune, or so it appears because the Lune certainly joins the Dee and Rawthey at right angles. The more southerly dale, the Dee cuts deep into the fell sides. Limestone has by now completely

H
2½m
4h
ooo
***

41

A quiet corner of Clapham

Whernside, the latter separated from the former by tiny Deepdale with its steep fell road over to Ingleton. The National Park Outdoor Recreation and Study Centre occupies Whernside Manor, a one-time shooting lodge. Courses are run on a regular basis in caving, geology, etc, and cater for absolute beginners to experts.

An ancient track, the Old Craven Way still links Dent with Ingleton. Climbing out of Dent as the hill road to Deepdale, it continues across the broad back of Whernside as a well-marked path before dropping down to the Settle-Carlisle line above Blea Moor tunnel. From the railway it swings to the south and makes for Chapel le Dale and joins the B6255, once a Roman road, down to Ingleton.

High up Dentdale, Deeside House Youth Hostel was a shooting lodge owned by Lord Henry Bentinck. Arten Gill viaduct above Dee Side House has piers which go 50ft into the ground to find solid rock. 'Dent Marble' can still be found in this area; once popular in Victorian times, the marble was cut and polished from a dark limestone to show its fossils which stand out clear and white in outline.

Linked to Dentdale by railway and road, Garsdale has no village or township, but dotted the length of the dale are farms which originated as Norse settlements, identified in their names; Knudmaning, Thursgill, Dandra Garth, Birk Rigg and Grisedale are good examples. At the bottom end of Garsdale is Longstone Fell, an unenclosed area of moorland popular as a picnic spot, which can be reached by either a path up from the A684 at the most easterly of two cattle-grids, or another from Lane Ends and over Frostrow Fells. The view of the How-

disappeared beneath the overlying shales and gritstones of these fells — outliers of both the Yorkshire Dales and the Lakes. These fells have a unique character all of their own.

Norsemen settled in Dentdale from an earlier invasion and Dent 'township' is a quaint spot, with streets still paved by ancient cobbles. Its famous son Adam Sedgwick (1785-1873), the father of modern geology, is commemorated by a large granite slab in the main street. During the seventeenth and eighteenth centuries hand-knitting became a major industry in Dent and surrounding villages; the special needles and the dagger-like sheaths used by the knitters have since become treasured antiques.

Dentdale curves round the north eastern sides of Middleton Fell and

gills opposite is quite superb and worth the effort of the short climb.

The River Rawthey quickly swells to a moderately sized stream with the mass of the Howgills to drain. Its town is Sedbergh, named by the Norsemen as 'Setberg' or 'flat topped hill'. The hill or hills being the Howgills which tower as a backcloth to this town of 2,500 inhabitants, the largest within the Yorkshire Dales National Park. The Howgills, green and smoothly-rounded, have a unique appeal and reward the traveller who takes the time to explore their quiet solitudes. This is an unspoilt area and, except around Sedbergh, accommodation is hard to find.

The Howgills, in particular one special hill, Winder, are well-known to generations of boys of Sedbergh School, founded in 1525 by Roger Lupton. It was originally a chantry school linked to St John's College, Cambridge, then in 1552 it became a free grammar school and gradually over the centuries it has developed into the nationally renowned school of today.

A market town since 1251, but never growing much in size, it was another centre, like Dent, for hand knitting. Between them, the two townships, in the heyday of hand knitting sent over 800 pairs of stockings to market each week. During the eighteenth century some industrial growth came to Sedbergh first through wool and then cotton. Behind the main street were houses some of which had spinning galleries, but all that remains of this industry is seen in the gallery in Railton's Yard.

The Howgills and the Lune Gorge, form the most dramatic scenery anywhere along the M6. They are a broad, inverted triangle in plan, with Sedbergh at the southern apex. Streams radiate from the central point of Brant Fell, all becoming tributaries of the Lune. Based on Silurian rock which shows itself only at Black Force and Cautley Crag, the hills have few walls and fewer landmarks. In mist the Howgills can be dangerous as the ridges and high valleys have a nasty habit of merging and turning to mislead the unwary. The hills are the haunt of buzzards and delightful wild ponies. In the deeply cut ravines and secluded valleys many interesting flowers grow. These are hills with distant views, to the west the Lake District and south-east the high hills of the mid-Pennines. Penyghent, Whernside and Ingleborough can be seen from the Calf, the highest point in the Howgills. Man has had little effect on these fells, using them only to graze sheep and ponies. A drove road came up Bowderdale from the north and crossed the high tops, but otherwise the few paths are comparatively recent. Hillwalkers who want to explore the Howgills must plan their routes carefully, for distances which are long on the hills can become vast if one is faced with a long road walk back to base. Most visitors will probably want to stay in or around Sedbergh and certainly the highest summits can be climbed from there. Anyone wishing to explore the remoter parts must arrange transport at the end of the day if doing a long trek across the high tops. The following selection of walks can be done either from Sedbergh or by using a car as a base.

Winder, training ground for Sedbergh boys, is signposted from the village as 'To The Fell'. Usually climbed as part of a longer expedition, but worthy of the odd hour or so to

H
2½m
1½h
oo
**

43

itself, the path to Winder starts from Joss Lane and follows Settlebeck Gill for a little way before climbing steeply up to the triangulation column on the summit. The descent is by the west ridge as far as the intake wall (a boundary between open fell and pasture). A left turn round the base of the hill to Lock Bank Farm and then Howgill Lane into Sedbergh.

H
7m
4h
ooo
****

A longer expedition and one which climbs the highest part of the Howgills starts from the Cross Keys Hotel on A683. Follow the signposted track to Cautley Spout, a fine series of waterfalls with a total height of 700ft. Above the Spout an indistinct track swings round above Bowderdale Head in a south westerly direction to The Calf. South from here across Calders and then south west to Winder and down to Sedbergh. This route as with most in the Howgills is tricky in mist and bad weather and for that reason should only be attempted in good conditions.

H
7m
4h
ooo
****

Another ascent of the Calf is from Beck House Farm on the Tebay road. Beyond the farm a path climbs easily to a col between Linghow (marked Far White Stones on some OS maps) and Fell Head. Turn right to Fell Head and follow the skyline round to The Calf. To descend walk back for a short distance and join the path down White Fell into Long Rigg Beck and on to Castley Farm and the road. On the way down from White Fell look back up to Bush Howe to the 'Horse of Busha', which is not some prehistoric symbol but a natural formation.

Parking is impossible around Beck Houses, but very restricted space may be available about three-quarters of a mile further on towards Tebay at Fairmile Gate from where this walk

Places to Visit Around Sedbergh

Kirkby Lonsdale

On A65, 14 miles north east of M6 junction 34.
Ancient town with many interesting buildings. Artificial water course along Market Street, once powered seven water wheels. Fine medieval bridges nearby.

National Park Outdoor Recreation and Study Centre, Whernside

6½ miles south east of M6 junction 37. Residential centre for the study of cave exploration and fell walking. Courses with duration of one day to one week offered to cater for novices and leaders alike.

Sedgwick Geological Trail

Longstone Common, Lower Garsdale (near Sedgewick). Meeting point for the geological systems of the Lake District and Pennine Dales. Approx. 1½ hours. Leaflet available locally.

Sedbergh

2 miles east of M6 juntion 37
Unspoilt town founded by Norsemen. Mentioned in the Domesday Book. Ideal centre for exploring the West Pennine Fells

Howgills

North of Sedbergh
Excellent walking area for lovers of solitude. Easy walks as far as Cautley Spout Waterfall (see page 33) and Winder Hill (see page 44). Rest of Howgills range virtually trackless and should only be visited in clear weather.

Dent

5 miles south east of Sedbergh on Hawes Road
Small village with narrow winding cobbled streets. Birthplace of Adam Sedgwick, an early geologist.

may be started by climbing Fairmile Beck to Whins End and join the Beck Houses track there.

Higher up the Lune valley, with the railway and M6 on the far side, there is a link with travel of a much earlier time. At Low Borrowbridge where Borrow Beck joins the Lune from the west, the Romans built a fort to guard the major route north from Ribchester to Penrith. Strategically placed it commanded natural ways south from high country to the north and west.

Tebay, as distinct from Old Tebay, developed with the building of the railway line through the Lune Gap and is known locally as 'Railway Town'. The long steep gradient of Shap Fell was too much for most steam locomotives and 'bank' engines were based at Tebay to assist trains over Shap. The site of Tebay village is much older and at one time the border between England and Scotland came through this area. When the Motorway Works Unit was built to serve the M6, it was necessary to remove a huge boulder from Galloper Field. This was the Brandreth Stone which once marked the boundary of two nations.

The original and much more ancient Old Tebay is on the bend of the Lune. At Castlehow there is a motte and bailey, originally defended by wooden palisades in the days of border warfare. The armaments seem to have been sling shot, and a number of iron balls have been found nearby. Old Tebay had its witch, Mary Baines, who predicted horseless carriages!

The north side of the Howgills is the least known part of the whole range of these little-walked fells. Tributaries of the Lune cut deep into its flanks inviting the fellwalker who prefers to walk untrodden ground. A long crossing to Sedbergh can be made if transport can be arranged. This walk starts from Bowderdale Farm (NY 678046) gains height on West Fell and follows Bowderdale to Bowderdale Head (marked as Hare Shaw on some OS maps). A right turn across The Calf and the path over Calders and Arant How completes the long route to Sedbergh.

Linking the Lune to the Eden Valley, the A685 road from Kendal swings round the end of the Howgills, picking the low lying ground to Kirkby Stephen and Brough.

H
11m
6h
ooo
****

45

4 The Northern Dales, Eden. South Tyne and Wear

Vale of Eden

The wild group of fells bordering Yorkshire and Westmorland are the birthplace of three deep and important dales. One is Garsdale and has already been mentioned; another is Wensleydale, yet to be described. It is the third and one which forges its way due north which we take first in this chapter. The river Eden rises on the high fells above Mallerstang and its upper valley has long been a natural way between north and south. Old drove and pack horse routes cross the gap above the Moorcock Inn, and the Norsemen came this way southwards in their search for land. The railway from Settle which has climbed over Ribblehead across the top of Garsdale now swoops past Ais Gill Summit and down the steep sides of the upper Eden before entering the valley's wider, easier contours on its way to Carlisle.

The oldest way into the Eden is by the bridleway known as the Highway, which climbs easily with little change in height from Cotter Riggs, in Wensleydale, to enter Westmorland by Hell Gill Bridge. The redoubtable Lady Anne Clifford came this way to Pendragon on her way to her other castles at Brough, Appleby and Brougham.

With the exception of the Highway, the only other defined path in the upper reaches of the Eden climbs up the steep side of the col between Little Fell and Wild Boar Fell before dropping down towards Ravenstonedale. Wild Boar Fell, a steep east-facing

escarpment is supposed to be where in the sixteenth century the last wild boar was killed in England. How true this story is can only be guessed, for there are a number of place names throughout the north of England connected with the wild boar's final demise. The only large wild creatures now are the occasional deer and foxes which are harried by local farmers.

A walk for a clear day would be to follow the path up from Hazelgill Farm to the col between Little Fell and Wild Boar Fell. Turn left and climb The Nab and its well sited tumulus to the flat expanse of Wild Boar Fell. If the weather is suitable it should be possible to continue round Swarth Fell following the county boundary, before dropping down to the road at Aisgill Moor Cottages.

Pendragon Castle was well sited to command the way through the upper Eden, but not much can be recognised now of the sturdy late-Norman pele tower. It was burnt by raiding Scots in 1541 but rebuilt to its present plan by Lady Anne Clifford in 1660.

Starting from Pendragon an easy circuit of lanes surround nearby Birkett Fell. These can be taken in any direction, but for the sake of clarity follow the route clockwise over Wharton Fell and then right to Croop House. Right again and along the river back to the start by the castle.

Kirkby Stephen marks the end of Mallerstang and beyond it the Eden meanders north-westwards through a

H
7m
4h
oo
***

L
4½r
2h
ooo
**

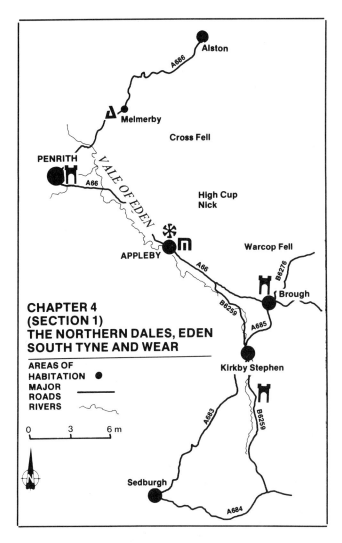

CHAPTER 4
(SECTION 1)
THE NORTHERN DALES, EDEN
SOUTH TYNE AND WEAR

AREAS OF
HABITATION ●
MAJOR
ROADS
RIVERS

0   3   6 m

wide fertile valley in marked contrast to its beginning on the fells. Kirkby Stephen is the market town for this north west part of the Dales. The church, with almost cathedral-like proportions, has many interesting carvings as well as memorials to the Musgraves and Whartons, owners of Wharton Hall, south of the town. Little now remains of the former glories of Wharton Hall, once a fair sized manor house, but most of the original is now in ruins and a farm house occupies the site. If you see parrots flying on a summer's day around Kirkby Stephen, do not be surprised — they are the hobby of a local farmer.

The A66 Scotch Corner to Penrith road across Stainmore follows more or less exactly the route of a most important east-west Roman highway.

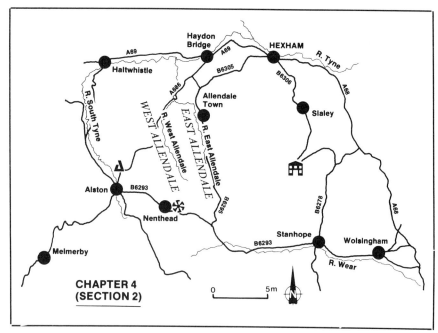

The importance attached to it can be seen from the number of forts and regularly-spaced signal stations which are marked on the OS map. The wild high country on either side of the road must have been a safe haven for the tribesmen of Cumbria and any Scots who managed to get south of Hadrian's Wall. It was difficult country for any military rulers to control and the garrisons must have spent many watchful nights and days looking out for fires signalling problems further along the road. Brough was one such garrison. The Romans knew it as *Verteræ* and sited their fort to separate the fertile plain of the Eden from the wilderness of the north and east. William Rufus son of the Conqueror built a castle at Brough in 1095 on part of the site of *Verteræ*. It was destroyed by the Scots in 1174 but rebuilt in 1204 and handed to Robert de Vipont, an ancestor of the Cliffords. Eventually their descendant, Lady Anne, came to own it and along with her other northern castles, set about its restoration after the Civil War.

Unfortunately the army have an interest in the fells north of Brough and as a result access there presents some problems! Few, if any, public paths enter them and any exploring must be carried out with a eye for trespass. The deep gorge of Swindale Beck which flows through Brough cries out for a path, but regrettably there is no public right of way alongside its stream. The nearest one can get to it legally is along the lane through Hillbeck.

Warcop, skirted by the A66, has many old buildings. The hall is Elizabethan and the church of even older foundation although somewhat 'improved' during the Victorian craze for restoration. Garlands hanging in the church are relics of the custom of leaving paper flowers in memory of girls who had died unmarried.

L
6m
3h
ooo
**

Beyond Warcop a riverside walk starts at the junction of the Sandford road with the B6259. The path follows the Eden below Sandford and then crosses the road at Blacksyke and climbs gently across the side of a small hillock before dropping down to Little Ormside. A left turn here and left again at a T junction into a wood, then left again at another T and over to Blacksyke again. Turn right at the farm road then fork left beyond the farm to follow a field path back to Warcop.

When it was the county town of Westmorland, Appleby was the smallest county and assize town in England. In the Middle Ages its population was much greater than today with the town protected by a loop of the Eden on three sides and the castle at its fourth. Appleby developed around its wide High Street which rises steeply from the church to the splendid castle on its mound above. This castle saw many battles in the Middle Ages, being captured by the Saxons in 1388 and later sheltering the locals of Appleby from marauding Scots. As with many of the others of this region, Lady Anne Clifford owned Appleby Castle and it was held in the name of King Charles Stuart during the Civil War. Sleepy for most of the year, Appleby wakes up with a jolt in June when gypsies from all over the country gather for the Horse Fair. This is when semi-wild fell ponies and others are bought and sold by judges of all grades of horse flesh.

Paths up and downstream from Appleby can be followed for a mile or so in any direction, but the return journeys must be along the same track for bridges are few and far between. The main purpose of the paths is to provide anglers with access to the Eden, but they still make for easy and pleasant strolling.

From Appleby Castle the view north and east is of the highest fells of the Pennines rising steeply upwards from Eden's plain. North of High Cup the summits are accessible to the fell walker. The army loses interest before the Pennine Way track from Teesdale to High Cup, but land east of the high tops forms part of the Moor House Nature Reserve, where free-footed wanderers are not encouraged. What is left gives plenty of justification

for the hardy fellwalker to spend hours of happy wandering.

A line of villages north of Appleby seem to huddle themselves protectively into the lowest slopes of Cross Fell and this is certainly necessary for a unique wind often blows down the western flanks of the hill. This is the 'Helm', a wind of tremendous velocity blowing from the north east, caused by a combination of weather factors. Cross Fell always indicates when this wind is howling down its slopes by wearing a helmet-like cloud which streams above its summit, hence the word 'helm'. The wind's strength is such that barns can be blown over and roofs ripped off. A delightful and allegedly true story told in Dufton, is of crows once flying off happily to collect nest materials with the wind behind them. On their return journey laden with heavy twigs they found it impossible to fly against the wind and

The glacial valley of High Cup

were seen walking back to their nesting places.

Of the fell-foot villages, Dufton is the prettiest, with its single broad street lined with horse chestnut trees. Nearby Kirkby Thore has a Roman camp *(Bravonicum)*, but Dufton on a bright autumn morning beats the lot. The Pennine Way comes down to Dufton after crossing some tough country above High Cup Nick and then climbs relentlessly up to its highest point at Cross Fell (2,930ft). Weary Pennine Wayfarers in Dufton might look despondent to the curious onlooker, but they can be excused, as they have walked a hard day only to finish south of their starting place of Langdon Beck.

H
10m
5h
oooo

Visitors to Dufton can sample one of the best stretches of the Pennine Way by following the signposted track from Billysbeck Bridge beyond Town Head. This follows a walled lane to open country below Peeping Hill and there is an easy path all the way to High Cup Nick. The Pennine Way continues across the moor to Maize Beck and eventually the Tees, but do not go beyond High Cup this time. The deep 'U' shaped valley beneath High Cup is a classic example of glacial action and the view down the valley, across the vale of Eden and beyond to the Lakeland fells, is just reward for the efforts involved in the climb. The return journey must be by reversing the upward route. On the way down you will notice a slender pillar of basalt slightly detached from the main crags of High Cup, this is Nichol's Last where a Dufton Cobbler sat and soled and heeled a pair of shoes for a bet. The 80ft high crags lining the edge of High Cup are of basalt rock and are part of the intrusive Whin Sill.

On the summit of Dun Fell, the southern neighbour of Cross Fell, are a number of aerials. These are part of a weather and radar station run by the Ministry of Defence. The service road at 2,780ft is the highest motor road in Britain and can be used by civilian cars to a height of 2,480ft, a factor which could encourage the faint-hearted mountaineer actually to climb a hill! Cross Fell itself is the home of a rare British mountain plant, the Starry Saxifrage — *Saxifraga stellaris* — which flourishes in boggy places around Tees Head, south east of the summit. Cross Fell in earlier times was known as Fiends' Fell as it was believed to be a place of evil. The name Cross Fell comes from the planting of a cross by Saint Augustine who drove away those evil forces. There is another Fiends' Fell about five miles away to the north east on the same ridge.

The stretch of Pennine Way over Cross Fell can be followed from Dufton but transport will be required at the end of this long hard walk other wise a long road walk at the end of the day could be too much for most. The route leaves Dufton at the right hand of the cross roads on the Knock Road, climbs gently by Coatsike and Halsteads Farms and down to Great Rundale Beck. From here the climbing is steep across Swindale Beck to Knock Fell where the walking gets easier all the way to the Radar Station on Great Dun Fell. Down 210ft to the col and up 191ft to Little Dun Fell, then down 229ft to the col and up a final 398ft to the summit of the Pennine Way at 2,930ft on the flat summit of Cross Fell. Walk forwards slightly west of north and down the far side to join the well marked track which was once used as a corpse road

H
15m
8h
ooo
****

51

from Garrigill in the South Tyne Valley to burial places in the Eden Valley. Turn left and follow the track westwards all the way to Kirkland and hopefully a car back to Dufton.

On the way down to Kirkland, ridges and terraces in the fields near Ranbeck Farm may be noticed. These are known as the Hanging Walls of Mark Anthony. Actually they have nothing to do with anything Roman and are older cultivation terraces probably dating back to the Iron Age.

Lead has attracted man to the Pennine fells and dales since pre-Roman times, through the monastic period when it was much in demand as a roofing material, and up to the twentieth century. Its heyday was during the latter part of the last century, when the industry became highly organised, especially under the ownership of the London Lead Company which developed a reputation as an understanding employer. The company realised that lead mining and smelting were unhealthy occupations and encouraged miners to live in smallholdings on the moor edge where they had enough land for one or two cattle and a pigsty, as well as grazing rights for a few sheep on the moor. Not only did this open-air activity help keep the miners healthy, but it provided them with an additional income. Miners lived in primitive lodgings out on the moors for five days and went home to their small-holdings for the weekend. Thus five day working came far earlier than we realise. The places where the miners spent the week are known as shops and they would travel up on Mondays armed with enough meal and pork to feed themselves all week. Sleeping accommodation was on straw-filled palliasses, and the lead-miners' life

was indeed a hard one.

The company agent for Westmorland lived at Dufton and for a time it became a place of importance as the administrative centre for the area.

Prospecting for lead, as with most other ores, is by looking at surface deposits and when these have been worked over it is necessary to go beneath. The local method of prospecting was simple but violent. A convenient stream would be dammed above the site under investigation and the water let out in one go. This rush of water would scour away the surface of the fell and the miners would then get a better picture of the underlying rocks to see if any ore was evident. The method was known as 'hushing' and bare hillsides around minor streams are usually the denuded remains of a 'hush' which took place probably during the last century. One example can be seen from the Pennine Way track to Knock Fell, where the unnaturally straight Knock Hush flows into Swindale Beck. Several major mines were worked well into the present century and the one below Great Dun Fell warranted a $6\frac{1}{2}$ mile aerial ropeway to get the ore down to the valley bottom.

Three ancient routes cross the Pennines north of Cross Fell. The first is the Corpse Road between Garrigill and Kirkland. Next in line is the Roman road of Maiden Way, a side road linking the major east west to north south routes in what was a military zone. The most modern road follows an old drove way across Hartside between Penrith and Alston. It is this road, the A686, which becomes blocked first during winter snows.

Beyond the A686 the Eden enters its final stage on its way to the Solway above Carlisle. The final outliers of the Pennine range are rather feature-less hills which continue to the east as far as the Newcastle-Carlisle gap. The Eden Valley continues to be an interesting place with ancient mega-liths, Roman forts and castles to give a spice to the landscape.

A couple of miles from the A686 beyond Langwathby and Little Sal-keld is the massive stone circle of Long Meg and Her Daughters. This is an oval 360ft by 60ft of fifty-nine stones each about 10ft high and an outlier, 'Long Meg'. A number of cup-and-ring carvings adorn Meg, the reason for these is unknown, but they had some great significance at one time. Half a mile away, to the north-east, is Little Meg, a smaller circle of eleven stones, two of which are carved with cups-and-rings and enigmatic spirals.

Using the A686 as a logical con-nection between valleys and resisting the temptation to venture through Carlisle on to Hadrian's Wall we can turn our attention to the valley of the South Tyne.

The South Tyne Valley

Cross Fell gives birth to two major northern rivers, the Tees and South Tyne. Although the latter, starts almost in the shadow of the Tees above Moor House Nature Reserve, it does have an important tributary, Black Burn, which drains the north slope of Cross Fell. The Pennine Way joins the Garrigill to Kirkland Corpse Road a little way north of Cross Fell, just above an interesting ruined mine. This track is followed all the way to Garrigill past the remains of several mines and is a worthwhile expedition from Garrigill. Nature has ravaged the work of the old miners, and their tunnels and shafts are now in a dangerous state, but the spoil heaps and buildings make for interesting exploring. Fluorspar, once discarded as useless but now in demand as a flux for steel-making, is coloured a pretty shade of mauve in this area and many attractive specimens can be picked up along the way.

Garrigill, which means 'Gerrard's Valley' is the starting place for a pleasant short stroll along the wooded South Tyne as far as a series of beautiful waterfalls. The walk is easy to follow and starts by the George and Dragon Inn, then follows the Tyne Head road for about a half mile beyond the village. Just before Cross Gill, turn left across the main river and then right to walk upstream as far as Ash Gill. Turn left and zig-zag uphill past the falls as far as the lane which turns left down to Pasture Houses. Continue along this track and across a ford where on joining the road a right turn leads back to Garri-gill. Just a word of warning, in heavy rain, or after melting snow, the ford might be impassable, but at least the waterfalls will be at their best.

The infant South Tyne flows gently past Garrigill, once the home village for Cross Fell miners and now much sleepier and smaller than a century ago. Downstream Alston developed as the centre of the North Pennine lead mining areas. The best walk from Garrigill is to follow the riverside route of the Pennine Way to Alston. The path starts on the south side of the river where the road turns sharply away. About a mile downstream it crosses the river and climbs away from it through the fields of Sillyhall and Bleagate farms before dropping

L
2½m
1h
ooo
**

L
4½m
2h
ooo
*

down again to the river 1½ miles from Alston where it joins the main road beneath the village.

Alston holds two records, that of being the highest market town in the country and that of being cut off by snow for more days than any other place — not a record to be envied. The market stance on a corner in the steep main street is rather vulnerable and occasionally gets in the way of heavy lorries. Lead is the reason for Alston's development. The market was created in 1154 for the benefit of the 'King's' miners, who had royal protection, but it would have only served the people who lived conveniently in and around the town. Farmers living in the scattered outlying farms only came to market on special days and relied on pedlars and packmen for their smallware needs. During the depression of 1812-31 when lead prices fell, the small-holdings were insufficient to support whole families without the men working in the mines, and over 2,000 people moved away in a short space of time. The London Lead Company's philanthropic attitude towards the workforce is recorded by such items as the Reading Room, which was built at a time when an artisan's ability to read or write was considered to be rather radical in some quarters. Smeaton's Drainage Level which drained mine workings five miles away at Nenthead was navigable by boats as far as Alston!

British Rail have abandoned Alston, but when the line was still open to link with the main line at Haltwhistle, two-coach diesel trains delightfully named *Bobby Shaftoe* and *Coffee Johnny*, plied up and down every hour or so. With minimal maintenance the line served a valley community and often during winter storms it was the only link with the outside world, but the authorities decided and that was final.

The Pennine Way runs more or less parallel to the South Tyne and joins Maiden Way above the extensive ramparts of the Roman Fort of Whitley Castle. This fort was a police post on the network of roads inside which Rome tried to contain the subjugated British in the uneasy *Pax Romana.* Maiden Way is clearly defined now by the feet of the Pennine Wayfarers and can be followed easily from Slaggyford north to Burnstones Farm. Cross the main A686 and continue on the Pennine Way until it rejoins the road near Lambley in another three miles. Turn right at Lambley to follow a path alongside the railway track to Whitwham and across the river to the hamlet of Eals and the road past Knarsdale Hall beyond which a field path cuts across to the road back by way of Burnstones.

At Lambley the Western Pennines can be said to come to an end. Coal appears at no great depth along the A689, coal which helped the fortunes of the owners of Featherstone Castle. The grounds of the castle are open to the public.

L
6m
3h
oo
**

The Far Northern Dales, Nentdale, West and East Allendales and Derwendale

The whole character of the northern dales differs from those only a few miles to the south. South Tyne, Nent, West and East Allendales and the Derwent are Northumbrian geographically and politically. The air is

Alston Market

different, certainly the spoken word sounds closer to 'Geordie' than Yorkshire 'tyke'. In only a mile or two an invisible border has been crossed and the visitor has entered the southern reaches of an ancient kingdom, for that is what Northumbria once was and the fierce native independence still holds true.

The River Nent is short, flowing only a few miles before joining the South Tyne near Alston. Nenthead was built as an industrial village by the London Lead Company, mainly in the nineteenth century. Traces of long-finished mining dot the hillsides between Nentdale and the West Allen, which, with its sister dale, East Allendale, is a quiet and secluded spot with little traffic to worry about. A network of minor roads and pathways gives unlimited opportunity for exploration. Most of the paths were developed during lead mining times and will lead the amateur industrial archaeologist on a voyage of discovery.

New Year's Eve is honoured in Allendale Town by a strange custom where 'Guizers', men dressed in a weird mixture of eastern and medieval clothes parade through the village streets with barrels of blazing tar on their heads. When they reach the Market Place, they throw the barrels onto a bonfire and after midnight go round local houses 'first footing'.

The last of five dales of the far northern Pennines, Derwentdale, cuts around Consett, with its sadness of the decline of Britain's steel industry, but earlier in its life it is a happy stream born in the wild moorland of Redburn Common. For most of its infancy the Derwent flows through a rocky tree-lined gorge known as the Sweep, before slowing into the artificial lake of Derwent Reservoir well-stocked with trout, and water for

Kilhope Wheel, Weardale

sailing. Edmundbyers to the south of the reservior has an attractive church which dates from Norman times although much of what we see now is the result of nineteenth-century restoration. Blanchland is a picture-postcard village rebuilt in the eighteenth century on the site of the abbey. Blanchland means 'White Land' after the white canons who founded the abbey in 1165.

Weardale

South now and into the County Palatinate of Durham, once a kingdom and still a Bishopric. Down Weardale flows the Wear, a river which like those in the Yorkshire Dales, has created a valley of character but unlike the wholly Yorkshire rivers it flows to the sea in its own right.

Killhope Burn rises only a mile or so away from Nenthead and in earlier times provided power to drive a massive 34ft diameter waterwheel at Killhope. This is the site of the Killhope Wheel Lead Mining Centre, which has a restored lead crushing mill, and is the area's best-preserved lead mining site. There is an exhibition in one of the restored buildings showing the life of a lead miner, and lead mining. The stream runs purposefully through Weardale Forest and Cowshill to join with Burnhope Burn below the village and form the Wear and so to St John's Chapel where Weardale proper can be said to start.

The spread of hamlets and small-holdings in Upper Weardale is typical of the way mining communities developed at the height of the lead-mining industry. The way the dozens of paths, like parts of a spider's web, wander across the hillsides tell of an area linked to a single purpose. From Wearhead it is possible to trace a linked line of paths downstream to East Blackdene and then climb up on to Carr Brow Moor to make for Race Head and a moorland track to Cowshill. Turn left at the road and in a short while Wearhead is re-entered.

Another walk which uses the relics of old industry starts 4 miles down the dale at Westgate. Climb the steep road out of the village to the hairpin

4m
2h
oo
***

8m
4h
o
**

Places to Visit Around Alston

Waterfall Walk — Garrigill
4 miles south of Alston off B6277
Pleasant riverside and gorge walk. See
page 53 for details.

Alston
On A686, 19 miles north east of Penrith
Highest market town in England. Interesting covered market stand in main
street. Excellent base for exploring the
Northern Pennines. Voluntary Society
hoping to open narrow gauge railway
nearby. Shops and railway information
centre.

Whitley Castle
On B6292. 2½ miles north of Alston
Fine example of a well fortified Roman
fort on the Maiden Way. Free access by
public footpath from B6292 at Castle
Nook Farm.

A side dale, Rookhope joins the
Wear at Eastgate and the only access
is by a narrow road which climbs up
the valley. Rookhope village itself is
dominated by its aluminium works.
Rookhope Dale was the scene of a
border battle which was commemorated in a long and not easily followed
song of thirty-seven verses. In the
sixteenth century Moss Troopers of
North Tyne and Cheviot ranged far
and wide in lawless pursuit of other
people's cattle and sheep. Thinking
Weardale would give them easy pick-
ings a hundred of them came over
from Tynedale to drive cattle and
sheep up Weardale and into Rookhope
Dale. A small band of locals pursued
them and a fierce battle took place on
Nookton Edge and the hundred raid-
ers were defeated by forty locals.

The discovery of iron ore in Weardale in the Middle Ages led to the early
development of small forges, but with
the coming of the Industrial Revolution there was an ever-increasing
demand for good quality iron. Ore
which was mined higher up the valley
at Cowshill and Ireshopeburn and
later in much of the valley above
Stanhope was transported to a blast
furnace built in 1845 at Stanhope.
Building the furnace there took advantage of local limestone, a necessary
ingredient in the production of iron
from ore and also coal was brought in
from the Durham coalfields further
east. As demand for iron increased a
company was formed, the Weardale
Iron Company, which built a further
six blast furnaces at Tow Law down
the valley. As lead mining declined
there was an ever growing concen-
tration on mining ironstone and at
one time 1,700 men were employed in
the local iron industry. From those
humble beginnings the north-eastern

bend and turn right towards Chester
House but do not go to it. A disused
railway track contours round the
hillside through Old Park to Rookhope. The return journey is either by
the quiet moorland road from Lintz-
garth across Scarsike Head, or if the
weather is clear, the more direct path
from Rookhope across Smailsburn
and Hangingwells Common.

Beyond Eastgate the obtrusive dust
from a cement works rises from a tall
chimney and cement dust covers the
surrounding walls and hedges, but
fortunately the majestic moors rising
steeply on all sides rapidly compen-
sate for this intrusion. Eastgate was
the gatehouse of the Bishop of Durham's Old Park hunting ground.
Westgate marks the western boundary, Northgate and the river being the
other boundary. Much earlier the
whole area around Weardale was
popular sporting ground for the Roman upper classes in northern Britain.

steel industry developed, gradually moving more and more eastwards and culminating with the massive investment at Consett. Now, alas, the iron and steel industry is temporarily in a state of decline and many furnaces and mills have fallen silent. The local dale's connection with iron and steel is still there in quarrying limestone.

As demand for Stanhope limestone grew it was decided to build a railway from the quarries to Consett and on to the Tyne. A glance at the OS map will give some indication of the problems involved. From the quarries to the summit the line rose up steep inclines some as much as 1 in 8 and the wagons were hauled by fixed engines. The route of the line can be traced alongside the B6278 Stanhope and Shotley Bridge road and ruins of the winding engines are still to be found. The line went over Park Head and dropped down to Consett where a deep ravine got in the way. Undaunted the pioneer railway builders overcame the problem by lowering the wagons one at a time sideways down an inclined plane. The line which continued to the Tyne was a marvel of engineering ingenuity. Much of the moorland route is now a footpath and bridleway, the Waskerley Way, but little remains of the inclined planes, the one at Hownes Gill near Consett for example has been replaced by a magnificent viaduct. The best way to view what remains of the old line is to walk up the B6278 road out of Stanhope and look out for traces of embankment alongside the road. Walk as far as the Weatherhill Engine which marks the top of the first steep incline. Wagons were hauled up to here by this engine along with another lower down at Crawley Side and then pulled by horses across Park Head. An interest-

A dales craft – stone walling

ing walk can be developed by turning off the road to the right by the quarries beyond the Weatherhill Engine House and cross Collier Law, then on to Fatherly Hill Currick and down to the A689 at Frosterley. To avoid a road walk back to Stanhope either rely on a bus for the return, or arrange to be met, or leave a car in Frosterley. Rowley Station near Consett, or Waskerley Station on the moors, (NZ 052454) are good access points for the Waskerley Way, with plenty of car-parking space.

Stanhope has been called the 'capital of Weardale', a high accolade for a small town, but certainly it marks the transition between encroaching industrial Durham and the wild fells on either side of the upper dale. Prosperity founded on its early lead connections made the ecclesiastical living wealthy and as a result Stanhope has had a long line of eminent rectors, eight of

M
6m
3h
ooo
***

58

whom became bishops. The church dates from the twelfth century and inside it are two Flemish panel paintings and a Roman altar found on Bollihope Common in 1747. As there are no evident Roman remains on Bollihope it is pure conjecture to try to guess how the altar came to be there in the first place, but a possible clue is shown on the OS map. This is the mention of Bollihope Spa a little to the east of Bollihope Carrs, (1,773ft) about five miles south west of Stanhope. One can only surmise that maybe there is a Roman bath somewhere around Bollihope Spa, they had a knack of being able to find suitable springs and Roman baths have been found in less likely places. Who knows there may still be remains waiting to be found up there?

The eighteenth century castle in Stanhope is a rather forbidding place, especially since it is used as a remand home nowadays. It was built in 1798 for Cuthbert Rippon, MP for Gateshead.

The tourist can be forgiven for thinking that Weardale is more of an industrial area than a place of natural beauty and certainly the eastern plain bears this one out, but it is easy to move away from steelworks and limestone quarries and escape on to the high moors. Two attractive side dales, one to the south west below Frosterley and one above Wolsingham come as a most pleasant surprise. Bollihope Burn does not have any rights of way along its length, but a quiet path drops down into it from Hill End which is above White Kirkley quarries near Frosterley. Waskerley Beck from Wolsingham is a much better bet. There is a riverside path which is approached from the church and it can be followed upstream as far as the road at Bishop Oak. From there the road which only serves a handful of farms climbs quietly to Tunstall

L
5m
2h
ooo
**

Weardale

59

H
M
12-16m
6-8h
oo
****

Reservoir. The return route crosses the Dam and returns by an easily contouring path round the hillside above Bael Hill Wood back to Wolsingham.

Another walk from Wolsingham follows the edge of the escarpment on the north western edge of Pikeston Fell. To approach the fell take the Hamsterley road south from Wolsingham and up the hill and almost to the sharp left-hand bend. Before the bend turn right along the lane to Carr's House and continue beyond the farm to a path which climbs the hillside towards, but not as far as Harthope. Turn right at the end of the lane to Harthope and follow the path across the moor edge for 5 miles to Five Pikes and Pawlaw Pike. Join the Stanhope to Eggleston road beyond some old mines and turn right along a path on the north side of Howden Burn. Drop down into and cross Bollihope Burn and walk down the road to Frosterley avoiding lorries from the cement quarry. With a bit of luck there might be a bus back to Wolsingham from Frosterley, otherwise it should be possible to follow the south bank of the river for most, if not all, of the way back to Wolsingham.

Downstream from Wolsingham heavy industry makes itself felt, even in this ancient town, founded in the seventh century during an expansion westwards by Angles under Edwin, King of Northumbria (616-632AD). Place names ending in 'ham' such as Wolsingham, indicate a homestead or a small farm which was built in a clearing in what would at that time have been dense forest. Wolsingham marks the end of the narrowest part of the dale for beyond here the Wear begins to meander south across the Durham plain almost to Bishop Auckland, before turning north towards the sea.

Places to Visit Around Weardale

Killhope Wheel
$2^3/_4$ miles east of Nenthead on A689 in Upper Weardale.
Well-preserved iron 'overshot' waterwheel fed by nearby streams. Exhibition on lead mining and life of lead miners in restored buildings.

Blanchland
B6306, 4 miles east of Edmundbyers. Site of thirteenth-century abbey of the White Friars. Village once fortified against the Scots, but now a mainly mid-eighteenth-century estate village but retaining medieval collegiate plan.

Weardale Folk Museum
High House, Ireshopeburn (A689) Small Folk Museum devoted to life and work in Weardale, with farming and geology displays. Interesting chapel next door.

Derwent Reservoir
B6306, 7 miles north west of Consett. Fishing, sailing, picnic areas. Pow Hill Country Park and Nature Reserve.

North of England Open Air Museum, Beamish
Off A693, Stanley to Chester-le-Street road.
A 200-acre open air museum of Northern Life. Includes a 1920s Town Street with shops, houses , pub, colliery etc. Also a working farm, NER locomotive and track, and other exhibits.

5 Teesdale

Teesdale is now wholly within County Durham, but with a flavour which relates it to the Yorkshire Dales. The Tees in its upper reaches is the most boisterous of Pennine rivers even though man has tried to tame it in its infancy. Cow Green Reservoir was built to serve industry lower downstream, and in so doing altered the face of one of the wildest areas of northern moorland. From its magnificent beginnings in the hills, the Tees eventually becomes the servant of man on industrial Teesside, but it just is not the same river by then. Fortunately we are only interested in its Pennine stretch where there is ample recompense for the horrors further east.

From Barnard Castle which marks the end of the division between fell and plain, north westwards, a quiet

motor road, the B6277, follows the river until they part company above High Force, the road continuing to climb to 1,862ft over Harwood Common on its way to Alston and the South Tyne. This road is a delight to motorists in summer weather with the ever-changing views which range from the wooded beauty of the dale above Middleton, to the far-ranging prospect across West Common, to the birthplace of the Tees high up on Cross Fell.

Tees Head is in fact a swamp at 2,532ft beneath the final four hundred feet of Cross Fell and is crossed with care by the hundreds of walkers who explore the Pennine Way every year. The area of bleak moorland east of Cross Fell through which the infant river threads its course is the National Nature Reserve of Moor House. It is

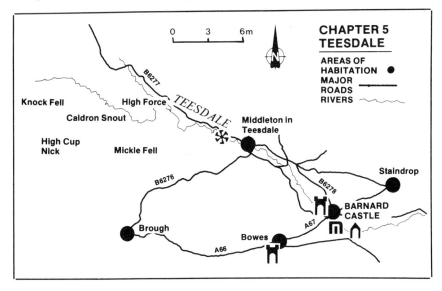

Cow Green Reservoir

an area jealously preserved and contains a unique collection of sub-arctic flora which can cope with the short growing season of about 165 days. These range from the Starry Saxifrage which blooms in the mossy places around Tees Head to the beautiful Spring Gentian (*Gentiana verna*) found lower down the valley. So special is this flower to Teesdale that a Gentian watch is kept by volunteers over its secret habitats during the flowering season. To see this startling blue flower is pure delight. Moor House, the house and centre of this preserve, is locked in a bend of the Tees above its junction with Trout Beck; courses are run from here and studies funded by the Nature Conservancy. Moor House is in a lonely and secluded spot at the end of the road which follows the South Tyne through Garrigill to its head waters.

Alpine flowers grow well in Upper Teesdale on a soil which is based on Sugar Limestone. This stone was made by the action of heat on hard limestone during the time when molten dolerite was flowing over the district to form the Whin Sill. Sugar Limestone crumbles into an alkaline dust, which when mixed naturally with peaty loam forms an ideal growing medium for delicate plants of what are usually more mountainous regions.

Downstream from Moor House, the Tees is arrested at Cow Green reservoir. When the proposal was made to dam this section of the valley the industrialists no doubt thought they had an easy task, for them this was just a piece of wilderness which no one wanted. How wrong they were! The battle to save Cow Green was long and acrimonious and in the end the ranks of Mammon won the day, but not until they had been forced to delay the construction of the dam long enough to allow conservationists time in which to mount a massive campaign to dig up as many of the rare plants as possible, and transplant them in suitable locations away from the shores of the reservoir. After all the heartache which went on before Cow Green was flooded, the man-made lake now makes an attractive foregound to the heights of the Dun Fells and Cross Fell beyond, but even so, it is man-made and an intruder in this place.

Immediately below Cow Green dam the dark coloured dolerite crag of Whin Sill has resisted wear from the river and makes an impressive foundation for Cauldron Snout. The construction of the dam means that Cauldron Snout can never again be the angry mass of cream and brown foam it once was after heavy rain. However, it is easily accessible by the road to the dam from Langdon Beck. Cars must be parked at Weelhead Syke and the road follows the side of the reservoir to the dam and a little way beyond it is Cauldron Snout.

Below Cauldron Snout the Tees is joined by Maize Beck and about a mile upstream is Birkdale, probably the most remote farmstead in England. Winters can be so severe and long that the farmer and his wife have had to buy a snow scooter to keep in contact with civilisation and more importantly to get round their land to check up on any sheep trapped under snowdrifts.

The Pennine Way path cuts a corner off Maize Beck on its way over to High Cup Nick and Dufton. Beyond Birkdale and marked on the map is a ruin known as Moss Shop, where miners would live for five days each week, sleeping on sacks filled with straw and living on a diet of oatmeal, pork and potatoes. Similar shops dot the hillsides all round the area and speak evocatively of the hard life led by miners of a century or so ago.

Rather than drive up to the dam car park at Weelhead Syke a much more interesting route can be followed on foot from the car parked on the B6277 near Langdon Beck. The walk starts

Cauldron Snout, Teesdale

M
8½m
4h
oooo

opposite the Youth Hostel and crosses Langdon Beck by the farm road to Saur Hill Farm and then by field path to join the Tees at Widdybank Farm. Beyond the farm it drops down to a pleasant stretch of flat walking on the grassy bank of the river at Holmwath. This does not last for long for the going gets hard over Falcon Clints, the continuation of the dolerite cliffs leading up to Cauldron Snout; this is a dramatic moment as the waterfall is hidden from sight until the last twenty yards or so. Scramble up the side of Cauldron Snout to the dam and follow the road back across Widdybank Fell past Weelhead Syke as far as the river at Langdon Beck, and follow it downstream to Saur Hill Farm where a left turn leads back to the road.

The Langdon Beck district is a popular skiing area in winter for north east folk. Access along the B6277 is usually good in all but the hardest conditions, for the road must be kept open throughout the winter as it is the sole link into larger towns for the whole mass of villages in Upper Teesdale, and even the Alston area. The main skiing area is usually on Langdon Common where the even slopes of the dry gully on Three Pikes provide good conditions well into spring.

A glance at the OS map will show what intense activity went on here when mining lead was a profitable business. Hushing, to wash away the surface was practiced here as elsewhere in the dales and the scarred gullies can still be seen, not overgrown after at least a century. A whole hotch-potch of field tracks criss-cross the area east of Langdon Beck, usually connecting smallholdings with the mines higher up on the fell side, the

---

Places to Visit in Upper Teesdale

Weelhead Syke Nature Trail, Cow Green Reservoir
Approached from Langdon Beck on B6277.
Scenic car park above Cow Green Reservoir. Nature Trail leads from car park across moorland. Opportunity to see spring gentians flowering.

Cauldron Snout Waterfall, Cow Green
Spectacular falls 1½ miles below dam of Cow Green Reservoir.
Access by footpath from Wheelhead Syke Car Park.

High Force
B6277, 5 miles north west of Middleton-in-Teesdale.
The River Tees drops 70ft in a dramatic spectacle of rock and water. Easy access by footpath below High Force Hotel, small fee.

Bowlees Visitor Centre
B6277, 3 miles north west of Middleton-in-Teesdale.
The natural history of Upper Teesdale visually explained in an easy to follow, yet well documented manner. Picnic site nearby.

Gibson's Cave Bowlees
Access by footpath and nature trail from Bowlees Visitor Centre.

Middleton-in-Teesdale
A small new town added on by the London Lead Company in the early nineteenth century to an existing, much older village. Used by the Company as one of their northern mining headquarters.

---

result of miners having their own routes, and an interesting couple of hours may be spent surveying the paths such as in the walk mentioned below. Not all are easy to follow, but stiles are the indicators to look for.

Hospital of St Anne, Appleby

The River South Tyne

Reeth, Swaledale

Langthwaite, Arkengarthdale

One of the features of Upper Teesdale is the number of whitewashed cottages and farm houses which stand out brightly against an often sombre background. An unusual practice in the Pennines, the custom of whitewashing houses in this area originated from a time when the landowner, Lord Barnard of Raby Castle was benighted while out shooting. He knocked on the door of a cottage which happened not to be lived in by one of his tenants. His request for hospitality was refused and he spent an uncomfortable night on the moors as a result. Not to be put out by a recurrence of this problem, he instructed his tenants to paint their houses white so that he could find them in the dark! The custom has remained ever since.

Using any of the multitude of paths near Langdon Beck Youth Hostel aim above Ettersgill Wood and cross the minor road by Etters Gill waterfall. At this point either follow the road to Scar End or use the field path by the waterfall and strike across the hillside to the old mine workings on Newbiggin Common (warning — keep away from any shafts, after years of neglect they are far from safe). Return by walking down the road from Westgate and at Watson's Bridge make for Broadley's Gate Farm and the path to Ashdub which goes by way of Causeway Syke. Beyond the farm cross Etters Gill and use one of the paths to Dale Cottage and eventually to the main road near Langdon Beck.

Two miles downstream from the confluence of Langdon Beck with the Tees the valley scenery changes dramatically from the bleak and wild

M
8m
4h
oo
***

High Force, Teesdale

open moorland of higher up to first a wooded valley and soon to gentle pastures below Newbiggin. The transition is marked most dramatically by the thundering of High Force. Especially after a spate of heavy rain this magnificent fall is one of Britain's wonders. Not the highest by a long way, but certainly one of the biggest in volume of water. In dry weather the fall occupies just one 70ft drop, but after rain another appears on the right of a dolerite buttress. This is a favourite vantage point and also one where quite often people are caught unawares when a heavy rainfall up the valley causes the river to rise in minutes and what was earlier a babbling rivulet can suddenly become an angry torrent. So watch for the signs and never climb onto the island if there is the chance of a storm around.

Most visitors to High Force approach it by way of the path through the grounds opposite High Force Hotel for which, or course, they have to pay. The view is worth every penny, but this way has the disadvantage that, apart from the small

Low Force, Teesdale

area of wood around the falls, no further exploration is possible. A much more entertaining walk is to cross the Tees below Low Force at Wynch Bridge and walk upstream along the Pennine Way track past Holwick Head House Farm and then through an area of juniper bushes as far as High Force. Return the same way as far as Holwick Head House and cross over the river to the main road; to avoid the mile or so of road aim uphill by one of the little field paths on the other side. On entering the lane beyond Ash Hill Farm, turn right and walk down to Bowlees to complete the walk. There is a good car park at Bowlees.

The waterfalls of Teesdale rightly command their full complement of superlatives. All delight the eye of the visitor and so it is not surprising to find another which is usually neglected and only visited by those who know it. This is the small fall in the valley behind Bowlees where Causeway Syke tumbles over the shaley outcrop of Gibson's Cave, the fall has cut back the shale so much that it is possible to stand behind a curtain of water and look out on the woodland scene

through a fine tracery. The approach to this gem is by the path behind Bowlees Chapel — it will only take a few minutes to climb up to the fall and the chances are that while High Force is crowded, you will have this one all to yourself. Causeway Syke valley is an ideal picnic spot on a warm summer day.

The old chapel at Bowlees houses a visitor and information centre devoted to the natural history of Teesdale, where grandparents can show youngsters how to use lead pencils and slates which were mined near to Cauldron Snout. The little garden outside the information centre is planted with a selection of local wild flowers and moorland grasses.

The first Wynch Bridge was unique in being the earliest suspension bridge in Europe. It was built in 1744 and rebuilt in 1828 to give miners living in the east side of the Tees access to the mining areas on the western fells. Probably it was the narrowness of the river at this point and firm rock on both sides which made the bridge builders site it just below Low Force. One thing is certain, the bridge makes an excellent vantage point to admire the spectacular rock formations upstream to Low Force and the tree-lined slopes on either side. The land west of the Tees hereabouts is part of the Teesdale Nature Reserve and as a result is out-of-bounds to the walker with the exception of one or two long-distance public rights of way. One of them, the path across Holwick Fell, was a drove road where cattle were slowly walked south on their way to market from the Scottish Highlands.

Below Low Force the valley widens a little and meadows appear on either side of the river, meadows which in summer are a mass of wild flowers which last until haymaking. The Pennine Way path follows the west bank all the way down to Middleton-in-Teesdale and with a bit of careful arrangement of transport back, the whole length of the Pennine Way between Langdon Beck and Middleton can be walked by easy to follow and well signposted paths. It is eight miles of the most superb and scenic walking, taking in High Force and Low Force on the way. The walk can be done in either direction but probably upstream is the best, as you will not have to turn around to admire the falls, but either way is highly recommended.

Middleton grew in importance when the London Lead Company built an estate village here at Masterman Place and opened an office to control their interest in the mines, which were worked until 1905 high up on both sides of Teesdale. It is hard to say exactly when lead mining ceased as a commercially viable enterprise in the dales as some small-scale mining went on intermittently until the 1920s, but it is generally reckoned that cheap imports of lead from America, Australia and Spain killed off the dales industry from the mid 1880s onwards. The Middleton area mines were about the last of the major sites to close.

A short car ride round the narrow lane which climbs out of Middleton above Huddleshope Beck and round by Coldberry Moor will take you past some of the old mines — **do not go in them.** Above the sharp bend beyond Huddleshope Beck are some fine examples of hushing and where the hillside has been washed away traces of ore-bearing rock can still be found. The track up Huddleshope Beck makes a pleasant afternoon or evening stroll from Middleton and the mines can be

L
8m
4h
ooo
**

Middleton-in-Teesdale

visited by extending the walk up Club Gill and then either follow the road or cut across the upper part of this side dale on a path which cuts out a corner of the road.

The Pennine Way route goes south into Yorkshire from Middleton across the corner of a long ridge running down from Lune Moor by the side of a conspicuous round hill with a plantation of trees on its summit. This is Kirkcarrion and is said locally to be haunted. How true the story is can only be guessed, but the mound had some ancient significance being the site of a massive tumulus. The valley which is entered on the way down from Kirkcarrion is the Lune. Not the Lancashire Lune but a much shorter stream and one which enters the Tees from the west. This river flows from the southerly end of the Cross Fell, Dufton Fell and Murton Fell range and in its upper reaches drains an area of wilderness uncrossed by any path and claimed by the military as a practice area. Traces of old mining

activity abound above 1,400ft and its lower parts have been dammed to make Selset and Grassholme reservoirs. Apart from the Pennine Way path there is little to attract the walker, but the motor road B6276 from Middleton to Brough is a delightful high level motor route on a fine day.

Downstream from where the Lune joins the Tees the valley bottom is flat and gradually widens with ever improving lush grazing, and so sets the pattern which is continued until industrial Teesside is reached.

At the height of the fortunes of the London Lead Company they built what was for the nineteenth century a modern crushing mill at Eggleston. With this they attempted to extract the maximum amount of ore from mines higher up the main and side valleys. Eggleston was more important in the past than it is today; since prehistoric times in fact. There was a stone circle here, but regrettably it disappeared when the stones were broken up for road building. A drove road came south from Hexham through Eggleston and divided, one section going eastwards down the Tees and the other crossed Romaldkirk Moor to join the one which came down to the main valley and went south to Stainmore. The bridge across the Tees below Eggleston Hall was built in the seventeenth century, probably before then stock and people had to cross the river by a ford which could be hazardous when the river was in spate.

On the other side of Eggleston bridge the road climbs gently to the beautifully situated village of Romaldkirk. The twelfth-century church of St Rumwald, son of a king of Northumberland, is set at the end of a narrow alley which leads off the large village green. Houses built through the centuries add charm and character to the place. Southwards across Baldersdale which the waterboard is determined to drown (there are now three reservoirs), is Cotherstone where the castle has provided convenient building materials for the villagers from time to time, as witness several cottages round and about, which are made from worked stones of higher quality than would have been normally used.

The Tees down to Barnard Castle is tree-lined most of the way and conveniently placed bridges north of Cotherstone make is possible to link up paths which follow both banks. This walk starts above Cotherstone Castle, crosses the River Balder and then the Tees. On the far bank turn right along the river bank and walk through a wood with the river close on the right-hand side. Where the wood ends the path climbs away from the river to West Holme Farm, turn sharply to the right down to the river

L
8m
4h
ooo
**

Barnard Castle

and enters another strip of woodland which is followed all the way to Barnard Castle. Return by way of the river's west bank, reached where the Romaldkirk road leaves the river. Turn right and follow a farm lane upstream to the disused railway. Go under the railway line to Towler Hill Farm where a path behind the farm descends gradually through a belt of trees to the river. Pass by Cooper House Farm and enter another group of trees, through which the path returns to Cotherstone.

The first-time visitor to Barnard Castle approaching the town from the south east may think he has been transported to France, but he can be excused, for the massive building which stands on rising ground east of the town and resembles a French chateau, was in fact designed by a French architect Jules Pellachet. The Bowes Museum was built originally for George Bowes, illegitimate son of the 10th Earl of Strathmore and from whom he inherited vast Durham estates and collieries. The foundation stone was laid in 1869 but George Bowes and his wife with whom he shared the ideal of a vast museum of antiquities and art, died before it was completed in 1892. Over the years the building became something of a white elephant until it was taken over by Durham County Council in 1952 and is now run efficiently as the county musuem covering diverse subjects from local Roman relics to the great masters. Galleries are devoted to period furniture. The museum is open all the year.

Barnard Castle is a venerable town full of delightfully interesting corners. Its castle was built to command an important river crossing and is named after Barnard (Bernard) son of Guy Balliol who was granted land here by William II in 1093. The castle was extended and strengthened several

Bowes Museum, Barnard Castle

times over the years and at one time was the property of Warwick the King-Maker through whom it passed to Richard III, and it is his emblem, the white boar, which can be seen on the wall of the Great Chamber. It is now maintained by the Department of the Environment. The ancient street names of Barnard Castle speak of the time when the town was a secure place and it was safer to be near a castle for protection. Streets with names like Newgate, Bridgegate and Thorngate radiate from the Castle. Thorngate, lined for part of its length by eighteenth century town houses, descends to the

---

Places to Visit Around Barnard Castle
Barnard Castle
A67 Darlington to Bowes road.
Castle built by Barnard, son of Guy Balliol in 1093 on land granted by William II. Easy access from town centre.

Barnard Castle Town
An interesting collection of venerable buildings lining the old streets which once were entered through gateways in a fortified wall. Covered market cross and Blagrove's House of particular interest.

Bowes Museum
In Barnard Castle on the road to Whorlton.
French-style Château housing a collection of national importance including paintings by El Greco and Goya. Displays of furniture and fashions.

Egglestone Abbey
$1\frac{1}{2}$ miles south east of Barnard Castle. Ruins of small abbey on a hill overlooking the Tees. Thirteenth/fourteenth-century nave survives.

Bowes Castle
On A66, 4 miles from Barnard Castle. Massive twelfth-century stone keep overlooking the River Greta. Built on the site of a Roman fort which commanded the eastern end of the Stainmoor Pass. Admission Free.
At the western end of Bowes village is Dotheboys Hall, once a notorious boys' school, now a private house.

God's Bridge
$\frac{1}{4}$ mile south of Pasture End Farm, $2\frac{1}{4}$ miles west of Bowes on A66.
Natural limestone bridge spanning the river Greta. Once carried a drove road, now used by Pennine Wayfarers.

river past an old mill and then leads on The Bank. Above it all stands the solidly built covered market cross, which dominated local trade when the only source of fresh meat and vegetables was that brought in from outlieing farms. Blagroves House, a sixteenth-century house, is three storeys high beneath a gabled roof. Charles Dickens stayed at the King's Head in Horsemarket when he was collecting material for *Nicholas Nickleby*.

From Barnard Castle a field path leads down through East Lendings to a view of the most northerly of the dales' abbeys, Egglestone. Founded in the twelfth century by Premonstratensian canons, this elegant abbey is the very epitome of holiness as it sits in quiet splendour above the tree-lined Tees. After the Dissolution, part of the abbey was converted into a farm house and several additions were made in later years, especially in the

seventeenth century. Beautifully carved medieval grave slabs dot the green outside. If you have followed the suggestion and visited Egglestone Abbey by approaching it from Barnard Castle along the path on the north bank of the river it will be necessary to continue downstream a little way to cross over by the road bridge. After visiting the abbey return by walking upstream along the south bank and cross back into the town by a footbridge.

Downstream again a path follows the course of the river into Rokeby Park behind the house, which is not open to the public. Rokeby was built in the Palladian style in 1713 by Sir Thomas Robinson, at one time Governor of Barbados, and he was known locally as 'Long Sir Tom' from his build and angular gait. On the eastern edge of the park is Mortham Tower, a fourteenth-century pele-tower, the fortified home of the Rokeby family for generations until it was bought by

Egglestone Abbey

Sir Thomas Robinson who altered and extended the wings which had been added in Tudor times.

The river which separates Rokeby from Mortham Tower is the Greta. Water flowing down it has drained from the wilds of Stainmore across which runs the A66, an important trans-Pennine highway since Roman times, as witness the number of forts and signal stations which are spaced across its length. It does not require a military mind to appreciate that here was probably one of their east-west lines of defence. Certainly it must have held great strategic importance as the link between the garrisons of Penrith and Carlisle to the west and York in the east. The ancient drove road south crossed the Greta on a natural limestone bridge known as God's Bridge and from there the route wandered south across Swaledale. Rokeby Park is bounded by the A66 which still follows the line of the Roman road to this day. The road by Rokeby takes a sharp swing to the south east away from the Tees and aims for the A1 at Scotch Corner. Hard by Greta Bridge are the earth bank remains of a fort and beyond one of the best features of the southern part of Teesdale — the wooded ravine of Brignall Banks, through which the Greta flows its last few miles before joining the main river. Here is another of those delightful walks where you can be certain of being able to wander without bothering about the crowds which can flock to better known but not necessarily better places.

From Greta Bridge follow a path on the south side of the river to Eastwood Hall and then climb away from the river to Wilson House Farm and on to Crook's House Farm. Immediately before this farm a short path across the fields leads to North

L
7m
3½h
oooo
***

God's Bridge, Stainmore

Wood, skirt along the top of this wood for two miles until a bridge can be seen over the river. Cross this, turn right and walk back to Greta Bridge by way of Brignall's ruined church of St Mary.

The romantic ruin of St Mary's church is over a quarter of a mile from the village and one cannot but puzzle over why it was built there rather than in Brignall. No doubt people tired of walking through damp woodland to and from church and in 1833 built one in a more convenient place, although burials continued in the old churchyard for another fifty years.

Rough pasture and moorland beyond Brignall Banks gorge is worth exploring. A complex of paths thread their way across Scargill Low Moor and are made for easy walking. The following are just two of the possibilities. The first starts and finishes at Barningham. Follow the Bowes Road west from the village and turn left along the first of two lanes on that side. After a quarter of a mile the lane begins to turn left, at this point look out for a path on the right alongside a brook. Follow this up on to Barningham Moor to a T junction with another path. Turn right (if you turn left it shortens the walk by joining the main route at Badger Way Stoop), but if you have not turned right, follow the path towards Stang Forest and at (NZ 045081) turn left on a path which climbs and then turns left across How Tallon. Here the route joins an adjacent way across the moor, passing Badger Way Stoop and on down to Barningham.

The second walk is from Scargill, hardly a village, but a group of farms above Brignall Banks on the Bowes road. There was a castle here once, but all that remains is the fifteenth century gatehouse. From Scargill follow the farm track to Low Swinston and then cross the fields to Gutters Farm and on to Garnathwaite (all lovely, ancient sounding names). At Garnathwaite aim for the back lane to Peak Hole and East Hope, continue along this road beyond Woodclose Gill and just before a sharp bend, turn left on to a path which leads directly back to Scargill.

In a wild and desolate spot on Scargill Moor is the site of a series of Roman shrines. The site is about a mile WNW of Spanham Farm (NZ 016101) and towards Eller Beck; the altar stones are in Bowes Museum, but what little remains of the sites can still be traced. The best way to find them will be to first enquire at the farm and then walk out on to the moor. As there is no path and few landmarks, do not attempt to try and find them on any day other than when the sun is shining and is likely to remain so for at least two or three hours. Of the shrines the first has a rectangular platform cut into the hillside and had an altar dedicated to the god Silvanus by Julius Secundus a centurion of the first cohort of Thracians. The second, a larger shrine is about 50ft away to the south east. This one is a circular stone wall and contains fragments of at least seven altars, the best preserved being dedicated again to Silvanus by Frontinus, prefect of the first cohort of Thracians.

A riverside path leads to Bowes all the way along the Greta and in fact it is possible to walk all the way from Greta Bridge to Bowes, but like all 'one way' paths it leaves the problem of getting back to the starting point unless you can arrange to be met, or are lucky enough to link with the infrequent bus service. If you can

L
7½m
3½h
oo
**

L
4n
2h
oc
**

L
4
2
o
**

74

Bowes Keep

overcome this problem then the walk is recommended.

Bowes is alive with the noise of traffic on the A66 but a by-pass is being built. It has stood here since the Romans built their fort of *Lavatræ* to command the approaches to Stainmore. Likewise the Normans following the Conquest built a castle here in 1171, but it was never more than a fortified tower. Little remains of *Lavatræ*, most of the stones having been used to build the castle and later the church, but the ditches and some of the ramparts of *Lavatræ* can be seen and from them we can tell that the fort covered an area of about $3\frac{3}{4}$ acres; from excavations it appears that the fort was occupied from the 2nd to 4th centuries AD. Water for the fort was brought by aqueduct from Levy (or Laver) Pool about two miles away to the north. *Lavatræ* was strategically sited at the junction of two roads, one running north east to *Vinovia* (Binchester) to join Dere Street on its way

north to Hadrian's Wall. The other road runs south east to *Cataractonium* which remains a garrison town even to this day, for this is Catterick, base and training camp for countless troops who have lived and worked here in the twentieth century.

On the edge of Bowes is Dotheboys Hall which featured in Charles Dickens's *Nicholas Nickleby*. Dotheboys Hall was a private school run by the sadistic and greedy Wackford Squeers who thought nothing of starving and beating his charges and whose education was his least thought. The character of Wackford Squeers was built on a real person who unfortunately was typical of his type before legislation came about following protests from such radical thinkers as Dickens.

An arm of The Pennine Way passes through Bowes before moving north again to Baldersdale and on the way

Bowes Chapel from the castle

cult lines in the country. Trains travelling west to east had to have an extra engine, and the story is that contrary to the rules which demanded that the train be stopped so that the extra engine could be coupled to the rear, to save effort the second locomotive would chase the train, and without being coupled would push from the rear. Dangerous but effective.

The main Pennine Way route follows Sleightholme Beck all the way to England's highest pub, the Tan Hill Inn. This pub has served well down the years, to travellers of all kinds from gypsies and cattle drovers to Pennine Way walkers, and more importantly to miners who dug coal from the many shallow pits which still dot the moorland with their open and unfenced shafts. The annual show of the Swaledale Sheep-breeders Association is held at Tan Hill on the last Thursday in May.

passes land claimed and neglected by the army. The Greta runs roughly parallel to the A66 and was followed by a railway line which, when it was in operation, was one of the most diffi-

From Tan Hill southwards the Pennine Way runs south into Swaledale and further east waters drain from the moor into the side valley of Arkengarthdale.

6 Swaledale

Narrow, sinuous, and always grand, Swaledale is the most northerly of Yorkshire's major dales. Its river, the Swale, is born among peat hags and heather over 2,000ft up on Birkdale Common, near the boundary with Cumbria. For its first few miles it is a frisky moorland beck, becoming youthfully exuberant above Keld, lively and increasingly mature in the next ten miles to Reeth, and never losing its unique Pennine character until its leaves Richmond behind and enters the Vale of York.

The enclosing fells of upper Swaledale are acid moorland with mosses on sandstones and shales. Plant life is limited, grazing meagre. Lower down, limestone outcrops as crags and scars around Keld, and with alluvial soils in the valleys, supports a richer flora. Stock find good pasture on the hill-sides and valley meadows, where lush grasses ripen sufficently in the short summer to yield a vital hay crop by July. No other crops are grown in Swaledale; its farming is wholly past-oral — sheep on the fells, cows in the valleys, with the occasional suckler herds.

All buildings are of stone — farms, barns, villages. Above Reeth, Swaledale was very much an area of Norse settlement a thousand years ago, and until the turn of this century some dales farmers practiced a method of husbandry still common in parts of Norway and the Alps, where a sub-sidiary house at a higher level was occupied during the summer, with sheep and cattle grazing the high pastures, while valley fields produced the hay essential for winter feed.

It was for this hay that barns, or

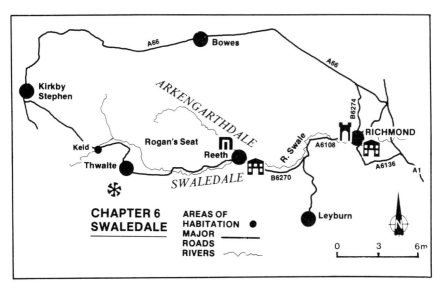

CHAPTER 6
SWALEDALE

AREAS OF
HABITATION ●
MAJOR
ROADS
RIVERS

0   3   6m

laithes were built. Nowhere in Britain is the pattern of dispersed barns shown so well as in Swaledale, particularly from Gunnerside upwards. Utterly functional, and placed exactly where they were needed, the stone barns were for storing hay above, and housing cattle below, from November to May. An average barn would store hay from one or two fields, and accommodate four cattle, and would be a small centre for foddering, milking, and 'mucking-out' during those winter months.

Swaledale experienced relative prosperity during the height of the lead mining industry and men of Swaledale were renowned for their skills below ground, skills which have been carried out from before the Roman invasion right through to the present century. Not only did they mine lead but a little silver was found, though never enough to be commercially viable. Coal was also mined extensively beneath the moors around Tan Hill to provide fuel for domestic use and lead smelting. Ownership of the lead mines had a long and complex history since the days when the Romans used it for waterpipes and roof cover. The monasteries which owned vast areas of the north until the Dissolution were keen to exploit the underground riches to help cover the huge roof areas of their churches. Northern lead was used on cathedrals all over the country and a thriving trade started in medieval times to transport pigs (or ingots) of lead great distances.

The village of Keld separates two faces of Swaledale. To the west the uplands are bleak and boggy, but eastwards the narrow valley is a delight, with its villages spaced almost equidistantly down the dale. These villages still serve as focal points for the hardy hill farms with their land on the steep valley sides, and common grazing higher up on the open moor. In spring the moors are alive with the cry of the curlew, a call so evocative of the vast open spaces of the High Pennines, above is the wind soughing through the coarse grass of the fells.

A multitude of small streams drain from Mallerstang Edge through the soggy mass of Birkdale Common and join together west of Keld to form the river Swale proper. Pennine Wayfarers usually use Keld as a stopping place. Keld, which means a 'place by the river' was first settled by the Norsemen but the village today owes much of its appearance to the lead-mining days of the last century.

From Keld there is a walk to Tan Hill which uses the Pennine Way route for return. Start from Keld by walking along the Kirkby Stephen road (B670) as far as Wain Wath Force and cross over the river to Smithy Holme Farm. Follow a rough path up the fellside to Raven Seat Farm and then beyond the farm turn right alongside the first stream from the right. Follow the stream for a little way and climb the fellside to the ruined shooting cabin known as Robert's Seat. Continue across this section of open moor in a north easterly direction across West Stonesdale and climb up to the road leading to the Tan Hill inn. The Pennine Way track starts opposite the inn and runs south past several dangerously open pit shafts above Stonesdale Beck to Keld, passing East Gill Force and Catrake Force along the way. This walk can be difficult to follow in mist so should only be attempted in fine settled weather.

As though to recompense for the bleak heights above, the river scenery

H
10½
5½h
oo
****

78

The solitude of Tan Hill's Inn

around Keld is a delight. Here the Swale has cut through to the hard limestone beds, which appear in dramatic steps, creating lively waterfalls. Of these, Kisdon Force is the best, set in a deep wooded gorge with wild flowers massing above on Kisdon Hill which separates the river's course from that of the road between Keld and Thwaite.

M
4¾m
2½h
»ooo

From Keld follow the Pennine Way route as far as the gate at the end of Keld Lane, then turn left away from the route down into the valley to Kisdon Force. Retrace your steps and rejoin the Pennine Way to follow it on a flat limestone shelf which gradually gives way to a path through high meadows all the way to Kisdon Farm. Leave the Pennine Way here and at the farm turn sharp right up the hill on a path across Kisdon Hill and back to Keld. This short walk (4¾ miles) travels through a wonderland and the view down Swaledale from above Kisdon Farm is breathtaking.

Thwaite is a little huddle of stone houses and farms which seem to crouch together in mutual protection against winter storms. Here again is a village founded by Norsemen, for Thwaite means 'a clearing in woodland'. There are not many trees now, but if the valley below Keld is anything to go by then this sheltered part of the dale would once have been densely wooded. The trees were felled to create farm land and never given the opportunity to regenerate.

Swaledale's most famous sons of modern times were Richard and Cherry Kearton who were born at Thwaite and went to school in Muker, the next village down the dale. Towards the end of last century these two did more than anyone to popularise natural history when the subject was considered to be far too academic for the masses. Richard was a lecturer and Cherry became the first free-lance wildlife photographer, filming big game in Africa and travelling all over the world in search of material. Photographing birds and animals in the days before sophisticated telephoto lenses and fast film was extremely difficult. To overcome their many problems, not the least being the need to get close to their subject, the Keartons employed many ingenious methods. These included the use, as a hide, of a stuffed cow, which often blew over in a high wind, or received the attentions of inquisitive live ones. Other methods were to hide in artificial tree trunks or boulders. They often stood on each other's shoulders or hung over precipices to obtain the shots they wanted.

L
2½m
1h
oooo

The short walk from Thwaite to Muker can be enjoyed by walking along the road from Thwaite in the direction of Muker. A few yards beyond the Buttertubs road junction a farm lane turns off to the right and swings gently up the hillside for a little way before dropping down to follow Muker Beck as far as the village. Cross the road, walk through Muker on the lane leading to Kisdon Farm, but turn left at a stile by the last building in the village and follow a field path through flowery meadows back to Thwaite. Try this walk in July just before haymaking, but please keep to the path and do not flatten the grass — it makes it hard to cut.

High up on the eastern side of Shunner Fell and almost at the summit of the Muker-Hawes roads are the Buttertubs, a series of deep holes easily accessible from the road. They are deep enough to break the bones of anyone foolish enough to wander carelessly on their brink, and fall, but shallow enough to see the shade-loving harts-tongue and other ferns which live in them. The technical term for the buttertubs is 'swallow hole' and perhaps this is an apt description of them as they have been formed by the action of water dissolving parts of the limestone strata. Frost action, followed by more water, has made what we see today.

The Buttertubs can be visited either by car or on foot. The walk to them

Buttertubs

starts in Thwaite and follows the Pennine Way along a walled lane which starts 200yd up the Keld road from Thwaite. After about a mile of steady climbing the walled lane gives way to a track marked by cairns which leads to the top of Great Shunner Fell. At this point abandon the Pennine Way and turn left to follow the watershed in a south easterly direction as far as the Hawes road and hopefully to find the Buttertubs. The secret of this careful piece of route finding will be to resist any temptation to wander down streams right or left of the watershed until the road comes into sight. As this part of the walk is across two miles of open moor, do not do it in anything other than clear weather. If the day started clear in Thwaite and turns bad on Shunner Fell, please turn back! The return journey from the Buttertubs is easy and goes all the way by road with breathtaking views of Swaledale.

Muker is another Norse settlement, but it is built on earlier foundations, for a number of Neolithic artefacts have been unearthed from time to time around the village. The church is sixteenth century and corpses were brought to its burial ground from most of the upper dale. Prior to 1580 when it was built, all burials were at Grinton and the dead had to be carried along a special route known as the Corpse Way. Parts of this road still exist on both banks of the Swale. An especially well-preserved section is the path from Keld to Muker over Kisdon hill. Most of the original character of Muker church was lost by eighteenth and nineteenth century alterations, but it did not lose any of its charm and it is a focal point of the village.

Muker is especially proud of its band which was formed in 1879. Brass

Muker

bands seem to have been a feature of the old lead-mining villages and were encouraged by the lead companies, especially the London (Quaker) Lead Company who set their employees' welfare high in their priorities.

Downstream from Muker short tributary valleys branch off at almost regular intervals north and south. Some are traversed by roads, others by paths, but all are of interest and worth exploring. This is where the true unspoilt character of the dales is still to be found. Oxnop is such a valley, a gill dale where mountain ash, scrub birch, hawthorn, holly and willow fill the sheltered ravine echoing a time before man began to dominate the landscape. The wood was a favourite hunting ground for the Keartons in their search for wildlife subjects. A path skirts the boundary of the woodland and starts at Oxnop Hall climbing to High Oxnop before crossing to the east side of the dale and descending via Gill Head.

Above the head of Oxnop Gill the open moorland of Askrigg Common can be explored from a carefully parked car. To the east and west of the highest point on the road a number of beacons are marked on the OS map. Although their origins are not certain it is possible that they were constructed by shepherds or farmers as guides or boundaries.

Below Oxnop Hall the Swale is spanned by Ivelet Bridge, an excellent example of a packhorse bridge which carries an ancient track across to Gunnerside. This name comes from old Norse and means 'Gunner's Pasture'. Above the village to the north Old Gang mines were one of the most famous of all the lead-mining complexes in the dales.

Gunnerside is at the foot of Gunnerside Gill which rises beneath Rogan's Seat about six miles away. Gunnerside Gill is a living museum of lead mining and two moorland tracks which follow its edges served the complex almost self-supporting industry. The valley sides are scarred with the results of repeated hushings which have left alluvial fans of debris at the foot of the slope. Two smelt mills, Lownathwaite and Blakethwaite were worked well into the late nineteenth century. Spoil-heaps and the remains of various buildings associated with mining activity can readily be seen.

There is an excellent traverse of the top of Gunnerside Gill's ravine. This walk starts from Gunnerside village and climbs steeply up towards Gunnerside Pasture above Birkbeck Wood, and levels out on Silver Hill above the ruins of Lownathwaite Smelt Mill. Keeping at a fairly level angle the track eventually joins the gill at some ruined buildings. The return journey is on the east side of Gunnerside Gill and starts as a footpath before joining a mine road down to the small farmsteads above Gunnerside village.

H
8m
4h
ooo
**

A high-level path joins Gunnerside to Low Row and Feetham, adjoining villages which have almost merged, but which retain individual character. Thomas Armstrong, the Yorkshire novelist, lived here, and his book, *Adam Brunskill,* is based on lead-mining in this part of Swaledale during the second half of last century.

Healaugh was originally a Saxon dwelling place in a forest clearing and serves as a suitable base for exploring Hard Level Gill where one of the most famous and productive mining complexes can be seen. This is the Old Gang mining field and it is possible to get within a mile or so of it by car. Start

Gunnerside in Swaledale

Places to Visit Around Upper Swaledale

Kisdon Force
½ mile south east of Keld on B6270.
Waterfall in wooded gorge. Approached by an easy footpath from Keld. See page 79 for details.

Thwaite
At junction of Hawes and B6270 roads, in Upper Swaledale. Typical dales' village of Norse origin.

Buttertubs
2½ miles south of Thwaite on Hawes road, near top of the pass.
Shallow pot holes on the hillside on both sides of the road. Car parking and explanatory plaque.

Arkengarthdale
Above Reeth on B6270
Remains of mining activity with ruined smelt-mills, flues, hushes, powder house. Pleasant short walks take in most of these features. See pages 76, 83, 84 for details.

Reeth
A once important lead mining centre. Attractive houses and inns surround a pleasant village green. Swaledale Folk Museum at Reeth Green depicts life in Swaledale in bygone days, including lead mining, farming, and village life.

Grinton
The church is often claimed to be the 'Cathedral of the Dales' and was originally Norman.

Marrick Priory
Ruins set by a wooded stretch of the Swale. Reached by a stone causeway from Marrick village ½ mile away.

Richmond
Ancient market town and guardian of the northern dales. The castle was built in 1071 by Alan Rufus. The keep is one of the tallest in England.
Green Howards Regimental Museum, Trinity Church Square. Georgian Theatre and Theatre Museum, Victoria Road. Still a working theatre.

either from Feetham or Healaugh and climb above Kearton past the farmsteads perched on a terrace high above the Swale. Park the car conveniently near Hard Level Gill and walk up the valley. Even though all is now in ruins, it is easy to pick out the various buildings from their foundations. The mines were owned by a variety of persons and companies through more than a hundred and fifty years. Lead ore dug out of the Old Gang mines was processed entirely within the confines of Hard Level Gill before being carried out of the dale by pack horse trains.

One of the attractive qualities of Upper Swaledale is its ability to allow the pedestrian to walk all the way from Keld to Grinton by riverside footpaths. Except where the road touches the river bank, a public footpath exists all the way down the valley. From Keld to Muker paths exist on both sides of the south-flowing river, but from Muker onwards the path keeps mainly to the north bank.

Early man left his mark with a giant earthwork at Maiden Castle and its attendant tumuli and dikes on the fellside opposite Healaugh and Reeth. Theories abound, but no real answer can be offered about its original purpose. One can only stand in awe at the tremendous labours involved in such huge earth-moving schemes.

An impression of Swaledale life in the heyday of lead mining is displayed in the Swaledale Folk Museum on Reeth Green, Reeth. The museum not only covers the history of lead mining in the locality, but also highlights social conditions of bygone days from the point of view of the farming community as well as the mining.

In Saxon times Reeth was only a settlement on the forest edge, but by the time of the Norman Conquest it had grown sufficently in importance to be noted in the Domesday Book. Later it became a centre for hand knitting and the local lead industry was controlled from here, but it was always a market town for the local farming community. Its eighteenth century houses and hotels clustered around the triangular village green make it one of the honeypots of the dales. Down the ages, Reeth has been a bustling place, in the middle of the nineteenth century there were seven fairs and a weekly market. Now the streets around the green can be packed with cars on a fine summer day, and in early autumn an annual show and sheep sales are held on the meadows below the town.

Reeth has its own hill, Calver Hill, the highest point on Reeth Low Moor. A shapely mass for these parts, it can be climbed direct from the track starting as a farm lane to Riddings off the Healaugh road. The path, which does not actually cross the summit of Calver, can be used to link up with one leading down into Arkengarthdale. A left turn at the road to Arkle Town and then right to a field path alongside Arkle Beck back to Reeth.

M
6m
3h
ooo
**

Arkengarthdale has one of the first dales roads to be turnpiked, that coming down the valley from Tan Hill to Reeth. It was originally part of a drove road which came south from Teesdale to Tan Hill then down Arkengarthdale as far as Langthwaite before climbing over Reeth Moor to Feetham. From here it continued south to Askrigg in Wensleydale and on to the Roman road across Cam Fell into Ribblesdale. The reason for improving this road into Arkengarthdale in 1741 was to help move the coal

Angram in Swaledale

mined around Tan Hill down into the lower part of Arkengarthdale, where it was used to fuel the smelting furnaces around Langthwaite.

If there is one dale where the whole story of lead mining can be seen from mine to smelt mill then Arkengarthdale is it. As we have mentioned earlier the museum at Reeth tells everything in graphic form, but the true museum is to be found here both above and beneath the dale. Hushes scar the dale sides, levels where the mines were driven either horizontally or at an angle from the middle slopes, deep shafts open dangerously on the upper fells and ruined crushing mills and smelting mills dot the valley floor. All this was fuelled by the coal of Tan Hill. Most of the mines were owned by Charles Bathurst and his descendants who operated as the CB Company. The only surviving roofed building from this complex is the little powder-house in a field by the road-junction west of the CB Hotel. It dates from about 1807.

The townships of Arkengarthdale were founded before mining came to dominate the dale. Arkle Town was a Norse settlement which gave its name to the dale, but the main village is Langthwaite, whose church, however, is one of the Commissioners' churches built soon after Waterloo. Above it is the delightful Georgian-styled CB Hotel. Across the valley is the pretty hamlet of Booze. There is no pub, and the name means 'the house by the curve' — there are no connections with inns or drunkeness!

There are old miners' tracks on both sides of the upper valley which will give the walker ample scope especially when used to explore the mining remains, but the road from Reeth to Tan Hill is probably the best way of exploring Arkengarthdale.

Rich deposits of lead were worked

on the opposite side of the Swale from Arkengarthdale. These are mostly centred on a broad swathe above Grinton where the inevitable scars left by hushing and other mining debris cover the fellsides.

In early times Grinton was the centre of Swaledale, with the only consecrated ground. Corpses brought down to it from the upper dale were carried in a wicker basket by relays of men from each village through which it passed. The corpse road can still be traced for most of its 12 miles as a path from Keld and it contours above the present road past Gunnerside and Feetham before dropping down into the valley bottom at Healaugh and Reeth. The custom continued until 1586 when the Muker burial ground was consecrated. Grinton church, which has often been referred to as the 'Cathedral of the Dales', was originally Norman but has been added to in the thirteenth and fourteenth centuries. Of its many interesting features, perhaps the best is the 'Leper's Squint' where people with this dreadful affliction were able to watch the service without actually coming into contact with the rest of the congregation.

Man has lived a long time around Grinton, the many tumuli and earthworks surrounding the village all indicate a great involvement with some force either political or religious, but none have had as much effort put into them as the huge dike which in complex shapes forms what appears to be a barrier between Grinton Gill and Maiden Castle. Roman remains were found hereabouts giving rise to the thought of battles between the invaders and local tribes. One wonders if this dike was some form of enclosure and connected with the enigmatic earth circle of Maiden Castle.

A fairly long walk can be planned to take in some of the mine relics as well as the ancient earthworks above Grinton. This starts on the road out of Grinton towards Wensleydale. At the first bend above the village turn right along the north-west side of Grinton Gill and climb away from the gill towards a junction of five paths on Harkerside Moor. Take the one climbing up on to High Harker Hill. Look over your right shoulder to Maiden Castle below and behind to the earthworks. Left are a series of hushes at Grovebeck. Continue along this path and descend a little way by a complex of hush debris, contour around the hill and eventually climb leftwards on to Whitaside Moor. This section of the route climbs gently across the moor and descends to follow Apedale Beck past a series of mine shafts and levels as far as a cross roads of paths above an old shooting hut. Turn left here and climb Greets Hill before joining the Wensleydale road back to Grinton. Throughout this walk you will encounter dozens of old shafts, but on no account go near the edge of any of them as they are all unsafe.

In Cogden Beck above Grinton stands the remains of a smelt mill built by The London Lead Company about 1840. The best way to reach these interesting ruins is by a path which follows the course of Cogden Beck from the sharp hair pin bend a half mile above Grinton Lodge. The whole of this valley is scarred with the remains of hushing and an hour or so may be spent picking over the stones to find samples of lead ore, fluorspar and other minerals. From the mill continue up onto the moor before swinging round to the left and rejoin the road beyond the old Wellington Vein mine and a group of limekilns.

H
12m
6h
ooo
★★★★

After all the wanderings in and around Swaledale's mining past a complete change of environment comes with the south-west facing villages of Fremington and Marrick on the opposite side of the dale below Reeth. Their history is almost as old as man in the dale. Below Marrick and originally reached by 375 steps, is the Priory a twelfth century Benedictine nunnery now used as a Field Study Centre. Further downstream is Ellerton Abbey founded by the nuns of the Cistercian order in the fourteenth century. Little remains of this nunnery except a tower and parts of the nave walls.

M
3½m
2h
oooo
**

A valley and fell walk can be used to visit Marrick Priory. This one starts in Marrick and descends the valley side steeply by the 375 steps through a pretty wood to the Priory. Beyond is the choice of field path or lane (but the field path is better). Aim for the Fremington road where a right turn leads steeply uphill to climb Garnless Scar and then another field path takes the walker to a point about a quarter of a mile above Marrick.

The main road from Grinton accompanies the river to Richmond with good valley scenery all the way. In contrast, the old road which climbs high above Marrick has more open views to offer in these lower reaches of the Pennine section of Swaledale.

Marske-in-Swaledale, although strictly in the side dale of Marske Beck, is idyllic, purely agricultural and surrounded by wooded hills beneath wild moors. The hall was home and birthplace of the Hutton family who provided two Archbishops of York, one of whom, Matthew, became Archbishop of Canterbury in 1757. Marske's church is of Norman origins, with additions in the thirteenth and seventeenth centuries.

On a high rocky crag above the Swale is a memorial stone erected in 1606 by Robert Willance to commemorate his survival after his horse fell over the crag in fog. Willance broke a leg and only saved himself by cutting open the dead horse's belly and thrusting his leg inside it to keep it warm. The stone can be found close by the prominent radio antennae above Marske.

The old road descends to Richmond, past Beacon Hill, which is an excellent view point from which, on a clear day the spires of York Minster can be seen far to the south.

Swaledale's capital, Richmond, is the northern gateway to the dales. The castle commanded all access in and out of the dale, manned by troops whose twentieth-century counterparts train at nearby Catterick. Earl Alan Rufus built his massive castle soon after the Norman Conquest and roofed it with Swaledale lead. Later the upkeep of the town walls was paid for by lead coming out of the dale, on a toll of two pence a mule load. Richmond became a stronghold in an area often under attack by Scottish invaders. Fragments of the old walls can still be seen in Friar's Wynd and at the Bar on Cornforth Hill. Legends link Richmond Castle with King Arthur and his Knights. A local worthy is reputed to have stumbled upon their treasure in a hidden cavern beneath the castle, but fled on seeing the assembled warriors. Unfortunately he could not find the cave again and so King Arthur and his Knights still sleep awaiting the call in England's hour of need.

As Richmond grew in importance it became the focal point for the commercial and agricultural interests of the dale and the surrounding area and there has been a market since 1155. Tradesmen settled and formed their guilds, some of which have existed in Richmond over 400 years. Nowadays the guilds are only interesting anachronisms which meet twice yearly for dinners and their only function is to appoint their 'freemen'. At one time the office of Freeman carried a number of useful privileges not the least being the freedom from road, bridge and market tolls anywhere in England. The local regiment is the Green Howards who along with the Royal Corps of Signals and RAF Catterick, can march through the town with bands playing and bayonets fixed. Their Regimental Museum is housed in Trinity Church opposite the Kings Head. The 'Lass of Richmond Hill', Frances I'Anson, lived in Hill House and was immortalised by Leonard McNally who wrote the song and married her in 1787. Richmond has a fine Georgian Theatre close to the market place, built in 1788 by Samuel Butler and restored in 1963, which gives a varied repertoire of plays and concerts throughout the season.

Reached by road, or by a short riverside path through woods below Richmond, is Easby Abbey. This Premonstratensian Abbey was founded in 1152 by Roaldus. When Henry VIII was carrying out his Dissolution of the Monasteries the canons supported the Pilgrimage of Grace of the ancient religious houses. They were shown no mercy and on the King's orders the Duke of Norfolk attacked the protestors at Skipworth Moor in 1536, and many of those captured were later executed on Tower Hill.

Beyond Richmond the Swale meanders on through rich agricultural land of the northern part of the Vale of York, before joining the Ure on its way to York, and eventually the Humber and the North Sea.

7 Wensleydale

In sharp contrast to its northerly sisters, Wensleydale shows a more gentle face even in its upper reaches. Where Swaledale is narrow, Wensleydale soon broadens into lush pasture. Its mining activity was confined to an extension of the Grinton ores, so through the centuries Wensleydale evolved a distinctive pastoral character which makes it a particular favourite for many visitors.

The name Wensleydale derives not from a river but from a village. Indeed, were it called by its river-name the valley should really be Yoredale, but today the river is known as the Ure, which rises among the lonely mosses and grasses of Abbotside Common, above the eastern edge of Mallerstang. After a short southwards flow its waters, quickly aug-

mented by other becks draining from the high fells, swing eastwards by the Moorcock Inn near Garsdale Head, and continue in this direction to beyond Jervaulx Abbey, where the more level land of the Vale of York draws it more southwards towards the Ouse.

Wensley village, several miles down the dale, was, during the thirteenth century, the only market centre in the valley, and it is perhaps this medieval importance which led to its giving the valley the name by which it is now known. Today, Leyburn, near Wensley, and Hawes, in the upper dale, are both market towns, busy centres both agriculturally and as focal points for an increasing number of visitors.

Several of the river's high tributaries, notably from Widdale, contrib-

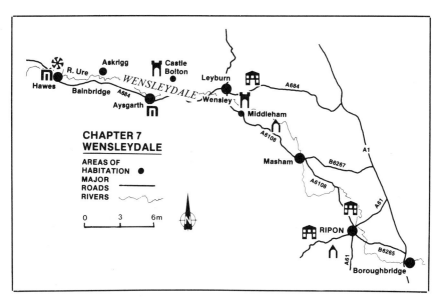

CHAPTER 7
WENSLEYDALE

AREAS OF
HABITATION ●
MAJOR
ROADS
RIVERS

0   3   6m

ute a greater volume of water, but a logical continuation upstream from the main dale leads to Garsdale Common where the Moorcock Inn at 1,063ft above sea level is on the watershed with Garsdale. The side valleys are an important feature of Wensleydale, each in itself worthy of separate exploration. Many ancient footpaths and bridleways link Wensleydale to the north. Lady Anne Clifford came this way when she visited her northern estates. It is possible to walk the length of Wensleydale from the Moorcock Inn to Middleham and the walk can be split into easy sections either longer or shorter than those described in this chapter. Each section will be described as a through route together with other features and walks.

M
6½m
3h
oo

The through route from Moorcock Inn to Hawes starts from the junction of the A684 and B6259. Walk north east to Yore House, then turn right keeping above the stream as far as the main road. At Thwaite Bridge cross over the road and follow a series of farm lanes and field paths to Birk Rigg. Here a path follows the river to Appersett. South of the village is a track of Wensleydale railway beyond which a field path can be followed to Hawes, thus avoiding a mile of road walking along the A684.

Appersett is one of a group of hamlets near Hawes whose name includes a legacy from the days of Norse settlement and farming. A 'sett', or 'saetr', was a place for the summer pasturing of stock. The other examples are Burtersett, Countersett and Marsett.

Widdale links across to Ribblesdale and forms a natural route for the B6255, with Widdale Fell to the north west and Cam Pasture and Dodd Fell

to the south and east. Widdale has its own tributary, Snaizeholme, and although there is no footpath out of the dale head, it is possible to follow Snaizeholme Beck all the way from the B6255 to Stone Gill Foot by right of way. The return is either by the same route or by the farm lane on the west side of the dale. This joins the road about a half mile above Snaizeholme bridge.

L
4m
2h
o

Places to Visit Around Hawes

Upper Dales Folk Museum
Station Yard, Hawes.
Exhibits of life on dales farms based on the Marie Hartley and Joan Ingilby Collection.

Yorkshire Dales National Park Information Centre
Station Yard, Hawes
Provides details of current events in the area along with displays to help understand the environment of the National Park.

Hawes Ropeworks
Near to Station Yard, Hawes.
A working ropeworks where handmade animal halters, church bell ropes, bannister and barrier ropes are made and sold.

Hardrow Force
1¼ miles north of Hawes. Behind the Green Dragon Inn, Hardrow.
Highest above-ground waterfall in England. Natural ampitheatre once held band concerts. Small charge for admission.

Semerwater
1½ miles south of Bainbridge. Access from A684.
Natural lake made by a clay dam left behind by the retreating Ice Age.

The Pennine Way passes through Hawes using a complex system of ancient roads and tracks on its route from Ribblesdale. It is part drove road and part Roman road across Cam Pasture and then a long sweeping run down from Dodd Fell by way of Sleddale Pasture on a delightful green road. It is these green roads which feature so much in the Pennine dales of Yorkshire. They are often walled for most of their length and are therefore safe and easy to follow — and stretch for mile after mile in solitude over the high fells of the Pennines. Invariably they follow the shortest route over high ground between centres of agricultural population. Modern transport tends to shun the more exposed passages and has left the green roads well alone, and apart from the occasional farm vehicle they are now ideal routes for walkers.

The Hawes to Askrigg section of the through route starts from the centre of Hawes and follows the Pennine Way south to Gayle. Take the Bainbridge Ings road, turn right along a field path to Burtersett and eventually the A684. Cross the main road by the lane leading to Cattriggs Farm. Do not go down the lane but incline right across the fields towards the river. Cross the river and follow the path alongside the old railway track to Askrigg.

Hawes has rightly been called 'the capital of Upper Wensleydale'. Its name comes from the Anglo-Saxon *Haus* which means a mountain pass, ie Honister Haus in the Lake District, a major pass between Borrowdale and the Buttermere valley. Hawes is one of the highest market towns in England.

L
6m
3h
oo
**

The Pennine Way into Hawes

91

Having held a market charter only since 1700, Hawes is a comparative newcomer but today it is a thriving little place linked by good roads to neighbouring dales, all easily accessible from the A684. Its growth increased when the railway came in 1878 and made it possible for Victorian tourists to 'discover' Upper Wensleydale. Since the decline of branch lines and the closure of what was scenically a most attractive line, Hawes station has been put to use as an Information Centre, and it also houses the Upper Dales Folk Museum where a comprehensive display of farm implements and mementoes of life in the dales is on view. The bulk of the collection was made by two women who have done much to record the past in these parts, Marie Hartley and Joan Ingilby. Industry in Hawes, apart from farming, has been specialised. At one time it was an important centre for hand knitted hosiery and for 200 years has been noted for rope making, a craft which is carried on in a long shed close to the station car park, producing a wide range of rope articles, including tethers for cows and horses. Hawes is very busy during the tourist season, with a weekly livestock market at its most active during sheep and lamb sales from August to October. Each year over 100,000 sheep and lambs change hands together with over 12,000 head of cattle.

Adjacent to and dominated by Hawes, the hamlet of Gayle is a much older place and is thought to be built on the foundations of a Celtic settlement. Wensleydale cheese is now made in the Hawes Creamery between Hawes and Gayle. Visitors to Gayle will be difficult to please if they are not entranced by the gentle hypnotism of the series of waterfalls where Duerley Beck crosses the limestone beds and ledges above the bridge.

From the top road out of Gayle an easy footpath follows the west bank of the beck as far as the farm at Duerley Bottom. The return is by the farm lane slightly higher up the valley side and it links in with the Pennine Way route for the last quarter mile back to Gayle.

L
4½m
2h
oo
**

Gayle

Places to Visit Around Aysgarth

Aysgarth Falls
¼ mile east of Aysgarth
A series of limestone steps create the Upper and Lower Falls. Information Centre, car parking, café, toilets, 2 craft shops.

Carriage Museum
Aysgarth, near riverside
A comprehensive collection of horse drawn carriages and vehicles as used by the country squire and his estate in bygone times.

Castle Bolton
Village and castle 4½ miles north east of Aysgarth on Reeth Road
Attractive village made up of houses ranging in two rows from the castle. Castle built by Richard Scrope in the fourteenth century, Mary Queen of Scots imprisoned here. Held out against Cromwell during the Civil War. The Great Hall and adjacent rooms have been restored and are laid out with kitchen and household implements of older times. Licensed restaurant.

Constable Burton Hall and Gardens
3½ miles east of Leyburn on A684
Gardens open to the public. Georgian Hall, by appointment only.

Middleham Castle
On A6018, 2 miles south east of Leyburn
Impressive ruins dating from 1170. Residence of King Richard III. One of the largest keeps in England. Maintained by English Heritage.
Open to the public.

Jervaulx Abbey
5 miles south east of Leyburn
The ruins show a fascinating ground floor plan of this once great Cistercian abbey. Several ancient gravestones and the remains of the fifteenth-century kitchen can be seen.

Bedale Hall Museum
Hall dates from seventeenth century. Georgian ballroom with fine Italian plaster ceiling and rare floor. Museum displays local arts and crafts, tradesmen's tools, clocks, coins, weights etc.

A longer walk around Duerley Beck starts again at Gayle and follows a field path and lane east to Burtersett. On entering the village turn right and follow a green road which climbs Burtersett High Pasture to Yorburgh (1,686ft). Continue forwards but where the track begins to turn sharply to the right leave it for a path which makes for the Roman road from Bainbridge. Turn right to follow the Roman road across Green Side and Kidhow to Kidhow Gate. There should be a signpost at this point which is an important junction along the Pennine Way. This is West Cam Road; turn right and follow this green road all the way across Dodd Fell to Ten End. Turn right below Ten End and walk downhill back to Gayle.

Pennine Way walkers leave Hawes by the Muker road and once over the river turn left to Hardrow where the Green Dragon Inn extracts from visitors a small toll to view the spectacle of Hardrow Force — England's highest above-ground waterfall (Gaping Gill and other pothole falls are greater, but below ground). The soft Yoredale shales have been worn back by the force of water and it is possible to walk behind the fall. At one time the natural auditorium was used for brass band concerts and the extensive remains of the old bandstand and terraced seats are still to be seen. These concerts have recently been revived as a popular summer event.

Visitors looking for an exhilarating walk can follow the Pennine Way to

Hardrow Force

the summit of Great Shunner Fell. On a clear day this makes an excellent view point. To the south are Whernside, Ingleborough and Penyghent, but the best views of all are those to the Lakeland Fells on the western horizon. The walk up Shunner Fell leaves Hardrow and turns right along the walled lane beyond the Green Dragon. Climb what is known locally as Bluebell Hill by this lane and after a mile enter the open moor where a clearly defined footpath continues steadily onwards up the hill. After a period of wet weather the upper section of the walk can be rather boggy, but the path should be easy to follow as it is marked by a series of cairns, the largest and best being that of Crag End Beacon. On reaching the Ordnance Survey triangulation point at the summit of Great Shunner Fell

H
12m
6h
ooo
****

(2,340ft) turn right and follow the feeder streams which lead into Hearne Beck. After a mile of quite difficult downhill walking an old miners' track will be met, follow it down the west side of the valley (your right hand side when walking downhill) all the way to Bluebell Hill where the walled lane of the Pennine Way leads back to Hardrow and well-earned refreshment at the Green Dragon.

Wensleydale, like Swaledale, has an old and a new road, but where the Swaledale roads keep swapping sides, the old and the new in Wensleydale keep to their appointed courses. The old in this case being the one on the north side avoiding a river crossing all the way from Appersett. While traffic hurtles along on the A684 life is more relaxed along the line of the old road. Askrigg is a tightly-knit village of seventeenth and eighteenth-century houses at the foot of its common land where the two roads from Swaledale join on their sweep descent below Green Mea. Askrigg was old before the Normans came and a market was held there until Hawes superceded it. As was the case in other villages around, hand knitting was a flourishing industry before mechanisation came along. Two waterfalls nearby are Millgill Force and Whitfield Force and the easy stroll to Millgill Force would make a pleasant saunter after lunch in Askrigg. To reach it take the lane behind the church to its end and then cross the beck by a signposted path and on through a pretty wood. Follow the stream as far as the waterfall. Retrace steps out of wood, turn right. Turn right through a stile after the first barn and right again at a disused farmhouse and cross a stream to Leas House and return to Askrigg across the fields.

L
1m
1h
oooo
*

Across the dale and on a tight double bend in the A684 is Bainbridge. The present day village is mostly on the west bank of the River Bain, and leaves the relics of Roman Bainbridge for some future archaeologists to uncover. What little is known of the fort indicates that it was an important outpost guarding Wensleydale. After the Norman Conquest Bainbridge was the headquarters of the forest wardens of the Forest of Wensleydale, who were charged with its protection for the king. The forest in this case was the woodland variety but gradually clearances provided farm land for an ever increasing population. The only link with the ancient forest is the custom of blowing the horn at 9pm every night from late September to Shrovetide, to warn travellers still out in the forest.

To the south, Raydale leads to a rarity in the dales, a natural lake. Semerwater was formed during the last Ice Age when a retreating glacier left a moraine, or pile of debris, which acted as a dam. So say the geologists but local lore has a much more romantic legend. This says that there is a drowned village beneath Semerwater, where a poor traveller, who tried to get shelter one wild and stormy night, was refused by all except a shepherd and his wife whose house stood beyond the village. The next morning the traveller laid the following curse:

Semerwater rise, Semerwater sink
And swallow all the town,
Save yon little house
Where they gave me food and drink.

Immediately a tremendous deluge started and drowned all the village and its inhabitants except the kind shepherd and his wife. True or false, the strange twist to this tale is that in 1937 when the level of the lake was being lowered in a land reclamation scheme, a bronze age village was found beneath the waters.

To see Semerwater, turn south from the A684 at Bainbridge and it can be viewed from the car on the road to Stalling Busk, or from beyond Countersett, but the walker who takes the valley path will have the best views. The path starts at the junction of the Stalling Busk lane with the A684 and climbs more or less parallel to the lane as far as the prominent hillock opposite Gill Edge. Views of Semerwater glinting in the sunlight open up as the path descends through fields to the point where the river Bain flows out below Countersett. The walk can be continued by following the lane to Low Blean Farm and then by a field path by the lakeside and on to Marsett. Return by the minor road through Countersett as far as Gill Edge Farm where another path leads down through the fields to Bainbridge.

L
7½m
4h
oooo
*

A more ambitious walk around Raydale from Bainbridge follows the Roman road as far as Bardale Head above Green Side. About 180yd down the Buckden road from where it leaves the Roman road turn left down the upper slopes of Bardale to Marsett. Turn right across Raydale Beck and then by the field path below Stalling Busk to Low Blean. Turn left as far as the bridge below Semerwater and then right to follow the path back to Bainbridge.

H
13m
6½h
ooo
**

The through route from Askrigg to Aysgarth leaves Askrigg by the Worton road and turns left along the lane which passes Thwaite Holme Farm. At the railway turn left to follow a path close to, but not on the former

L
4½m
2h
oooo
**

Aysgarth Falls

line (which is private property) to Aysgarth.

Limestone beds which feature so prominently in the western part of the dales, dip below ground to the east and north-east and in lower Wensleydale they are only visible as the river bed, but what an effect it makes.

Below Aysgarth the river tumbles over three broad steps in the limestone to create the famous Aysgarth Falls, one of the most popular picnic spots in the dales. Careful screening of the National Park car park ensures that the cars of the many visitors to the falls do not detract visually from their truly delightful scenic value. Paths to the falls are signposted and there is an excellent Information Centre by the old station. The power of the river was used to drive the mill, which now houses the Yorkshire Museum of Horse Drawn Carriages. Aysgarth's church is mainly Victorian but contains a medieval rood screen and bench ends from Jervaulx Abbey, by Ripon Carvers.

Bishopdale, another of the tributaries of the Ure is quiet and little known, despite having the road from Wharfedale down its length. Few motorists who drive over from Buck-den take the trouble to stop and explore its hidden byways, but those who do will be well rewarded. The three Bishopdale villages, West Burton, Thoralby and Newbiggin are clusters of interesting houses, most of them around 200 years old. Both West Burton and Thoralby have pretty waterfalls nearby and a complex of interlinked footpaths weaves in and out of the farmsteads on the dale's side.

The track which climbs from Newbiggin to Wasset Fell was originally used by the miners who worked the sparse veins on the fells on either side of Bishopdale.

The through route from Aysgarth to Wensley begins at the falls. Walk up through Aysgarth towards the main road and turn left through the churchyard to follow a field path which eventually joins the A684 at Hestholme Bridge. Turn left along the main road and then left opposite its junction with the B6160 Bishopdale road. A path leads down to the south bank of the Ure which can be followed all the way down to Wensley.

In late August the straggling village of West Witton lining the A684 has a

L
7½m
4h
ooo
*

Arkengarthdale

Wensleydale near Castle Bolton

Wharfedale near Grassington

Bolton Abbey, Wharfedale

traditional bonfire ceremony. The true origin is probably pagan and is lost in antiquity but is known locally as the 'Burning of Bartle' or St Bartholomew. West Witton was mentioned in the Domesday Book as Wittone, a stone village. Penhill to the south is an ancient beacon site, a point for both warning and celebratory fires. A three-quarters-of-a-mile climb from the Melmerby road leads to this vantage point with its views of Wensleydale.

Across the shoulder of Penhill is Coverdale, the last of the Ure's southern feeders, yet another of the often ignored places of solitude. The long valley road through its scattered communities offers a reward to the motorist, but great care must be taken on its descent into Wharfedale down the steep Park Rash. This road was once a pack horse way and the village of Horsehouse was a principal resting place before the long haul across the moors to Kettlewell. Lower down Coverdale, the ruins of Coverham Abbey are now incorporated into a private house, and nearby the packhorse trains would have crossed the river by the beautiful bridge below the church.

H
10m
5h
oo
***

Footpaths which in the old days were made to provide the shortest passage between two places can be used for pleasure today. Two which linked Coverdale to Bishopsdale are such tracks and offer an enjoyable day's walk across Carlton Moor. Start in Carlton and climb up the walled lane which is a continuation of the main street. In other words, turn right where the motor road from Carlton turns sharply left. Climb steadily up the dry valley and across Burton Moor into Walden by Cote Farm. Turn left along the road below Scar Folds for a little more than a mile

as far as the sharp bend below White-row Farm. At the top of the bend turn left to follow a green road which leads past the old mines of Fleensop Moor. Almost at the top of the climb out of Fleens Gill turn left across the moor and down to Horsehouse. Field paths parallel to the road follow the north bank of the River Cover back to Carlton.

The first road through Wensleydale kept well above the north bank of the river and wound up and down steep hillsides in a manner which would be unacceptable for motorised traffic. As a result the villages on this side have remained unspoilt with very little development over the years.

Up the road from Aysgarth the village of Carperby proudly boasts the fact that it has twice won the best kept village competition organised by the Yorkshire Rural Community Council. There was once a market here centred on the seven-stepped cross which was raised in 1674. Nearby in the fields north of the road can be seen examples of lynchets — horizontal strips ploughed along a hillside in medieval days to provide more arable land.

Castle Bolton saw excitement for over a year during the Civil War and it is nice to think that little has happened to the village since then of such a similar shattering experience. The castle which dominates the village was built in 1379 at a cost of £12,000 for the first Lord Scrope, a Chancellor of England. The ill fated Mary Queen of Scots was lodged here from July 1567 to January 1569 on her slow journey south and eventual execution. Colonel Chaytor held the castle for the crown against the troops of Oliver Cromwell until forced by starvation to surrender in 1645. The castle re-

Castle Bolton

mained unoccupied until recently when work was commenced to preserve this fine building. A licenced restaurant occupies the rebuilt section.

Across Apedale Beck Redmire housed miners who worked the veins of the south side of the Grinton ore field. In 1861 the population was 420 but now it is about half that number. Redmire takes its name from the reedy lake which was to the south of the village until it was drained in the last century.

Marked on the OS map as 'Old Flue' above Preston-under-Scar is the longest flue in England which ran underground from the smelt mill at Keld Heads to Cobscar over a mile and a half away on the moors to the north. Some of the richest lead veins in Wensleydale were worked around here.

Not shown on any OS map are the prehistoric dwellings which were discovered a little to the east of Preston-under-Scar. The road across the Red-

mire Scar has the surprise view of Wensleydale from Scarth Nick. Below the village, Apedale Beck feeds in to the Ure below Redmire Force, the last of the limestone-step waterfalls of Wensleydale.

The dale takes its name from Wensley, now overshadowed in commercial importance by Hawes, but Wensley is a far prettier place surrounding its ancient village green. The church is one of the most beautiful in the dales and most of what we see now was built in the thirteenth and fifteenth centuries, the date of much of its fine woodwork. Peter Goldsmith, who was the surgeon on board HMS *Victory* in whose arms Lord Nelson died at Trafalgar came from Wensley and is buried in the churchyard. In 1563 disaster struck Wensley when the Great Plague arrived and killed many of its inhabitants.

Bolton Hall has its main gates in the centre of Wensley, and there are public footpaths through the beautiful parkland, though the hall itself is not open. It was built in 1678 by Charles Powlett who later became the Duke of

Bolton, and was partially rebuilt early this century after a serious fire.

L
3m
1½h
oo

The final section of the through route is from Wensley to Middleham. From the road bridge below Wensley follow the south side of the river keeping to the bank for about a quarter of a mile, and then aim for a barn and the top side of the wood ahead. Walk down past a small pond to another wood and skirt the ox-bow bend in the river to join the farm lane to Middleham Bridge. About half way along the lane turn right and cross a series of fields to Middleham.

The through route may be continued by following the river bank path from Cover Bridge Inn as far as Jervaulx Abbey, but afterwards it becomes fragmented and thus no longer suitable as a truly continuous path.

Leyburn had its market charter granted by Charles I, and since 1686 Friday has been the day when market activity centres on this town which was mentioned on the Domesday Book as 'le borne' or 'the stream by the clearing'. From the west end of the market place a footpath leads to the wooded crag of Leyburn Shawl.

Middleham is linked to Leyburn by an iron girder bridge built by public subscription in 1850 to replace an earlier suspension bridge which collapsed in 1831 after only two years' use. The impressive ruins of Middleham Castle date from 1170, which three centuries later was home for the future Richard III. The keep is original and stands in a fine state of preservation as a true memorial to the medieval stonemasons who built it. Middleham is a racehorse training town with a dozen trainers handling several hundred horses, often to be seen at exercise on Middleham Moor.

Below Middleham the valley opens

Detail of the doorway at Ripon Cathedral

99

out and its character becomes more wooded. The ruins of Jervaulx Abbey are about three miles from Middleham on the Masham road. It was built in the twelfth century by Cistercian monks who moved here from the then inhospitable area around Askrigg. The monks made a special cheese, a forerunner to Wensleydale cheese, from ewes' milk. The scant ruins of Jervalux Abbey remain in mute testimony to Henry VIII's determination to crush the power of the monasteries. In 1536 the Pilgrimage of Grace started from here, led unwillingly by the abbot, Adam Sedburgh. The pilgrims hoped to persuade the king away from his policy of destroying the monasteries, but he tricked them by offering a pardon. As soon as they made to return to their dales he took revenge on them and Jervaulx. Adam Sedburgh was imprisoned in the Tower

of London, where his name can still be seen scratched on a wall. He was executed at Tyburn in 1537.

Devotees of 'real ale' make the pilgrimage to Masham for it is the home of one of the oldest and truest brews, Theakston's 'Old Peculier'. Masham guards a crossing of the Ure on its southerly course into the Vale of York. Its church contains some Norman work but has been Victorianised. There is a ninth-century Anglian cross in the churchyard. A market has been held at Masham since 1250, and the huge market place gives an air of spaciousness to the town. Downstream, noble houses set amidst their parkland line both banks of the Ure as far as, and beyond, Ripon.

Ripon's past has been closely linked to its church for thirteen centuries. In 664 Wilfred became bishop and rebuilt its first church soon afterwards. The crypt of this still survives, and can be visited, beneath the present central

Fountains Abbey

Places to Visit Around Ripon

Lightwater Valley Action Park
3 miles north of Ripon on A6108
Visitor centre, adventure playground, miniature railway, fruit farm, craft centre, old time fair, boating, gift shops, restaurants, fruit picking.

Fountains Abbey and Studley Royal
2 miles west of Ripon off the B6265 to Pateley Bridge
The largest monastic ruin in Britain; founded by Cistercian monks in 1132; landscape gardens laid out 1720-40 with lake, formal water-garden and temples; deer park; St ,Mary's Church; Jacobean Mansion House; small museum.

Norton Conyers
3½ miles north of Ripon off A61
Fine Jacobean manor house belonging to the Grahams, who still live there, since 1624. Exhibition of pictures, furniture & wedding dresses. Walled garden.

Wakeman's House Museum
Market Square, Ripon
Building dating from the fourteenth century. Residence of the 'Wakeman' or nightwatchman in medieval times. Office still marked by the sounding of a nightly horn and ringing a curfew bell at 9pm. Now houses an information centre and museum of local crafts and history.

Ripon Town
Cathedral dates from 672. Rich ecclesiastical treasure displayed in the Saxon crypt.

Newby Hall
4 miles south of Ripon off Boroughbridge Old Road.
Built in 1690s for Sir Edward Blackett, then redesigned in the eighteenth century by Robert Adam. Works of art, sculptures and valuable furnishings fill the hall. House and landscaped gardens open to the public. Children's adventure playground, miniature steam railway.

The gardens of Studley Park

tower. Today's Minster, raised to cathedral status in 1836, has one of the greatest of our Early English west fronts.

As a religious centre in its own right, as well as being close to Fountains Abbey's monastic influence, and conveniently placed between the pastoral countryside of Wensleydale and Nidderdale and the rich arable lands of the Vale of York, Ripon soon acquired charters for markets and fairs. It developed round the twin centres of minster and market-place, the two parts of the town most attractive to visitors. The medieval street pattern is still based on these areas, but most of Ripon's attractive buildings are the result of Georgian and Victorian growth. In the centre of the market-place is an impressive obelisk of 1781, and on the south side the elegant Town Hall of 1801 almost overshadows a surviving half-timbered building, the sixteenth-century Wakeman's House. One of the Wakeman's duties was that of Hornblower, a custom still continued each evening at 9pm, when he blows a horn at each corner of the market-place, and outside the house of the current mayor.

Fountains Abbey is three miles south-west of Ripon. Founded in 1132 on what was then a wild site by the little River Skell, it became one of the richest of all Cistercian monasteries. Today, in their setting of an eighteenth-century landscaped park, its ruins are probably the most beautiful and certainly the most extensive, of any Cistercian foundation in Britain.

The riverside below Fountains Abbey opens out into ornamental gardens and ponds full of exotic geese and visiting water birds. This is Studley Royal Park created in the 1720s by John Aislabie as a deer park near his house, of which only the stable block remains. Fountains Abbey and Studley Royal are now part of the National Trust. A short stroll which takes in the glories of the abbey and the beauty of Studley starts at the abbey car park and follows the Skell past Fountains Hall to the abbey, it continues down stream past Half Moon Pound and through the ornamental gardens of the park to follow the canal to the lake with its numerous geese and ducks both wild and tame. Up past Studley Royal car park and left at the cross tracks to St Mary's church and out of the park boundary. Turn left along the lane which will lead you back to the abbey car park. Although this walk is little more than three miles, it is one which could take all day if you wish. The abbey ruins need at least an hour to appreciate them and the grounds of Studley Royal are ideal for picnicing and observing the wildlife.

L
3½m
2h
oooo
*

8 Nidderdale and Wharfedale

Nidderdale

A short step across the moor from Skell Dale beyond Fountains Abbey and the character changes yet again in the shortest of the main dales. Nidderdale packs a great deal of interest into its length and provides drinking water for the densely populated regions to its south.

Approach the dale by the back road from Masham in Wensleydale, over Ouster Bank and steeply down to Lofthouse. Across the valley is the spectacular How Stean Gorge which has been developed as a visitor centre.

Footbridges on different levels allow access across the deep chasm and there is a childrens' play area nearby. A visit to How Stean Gorge can be extended by a short walk along the side of the gorge as far as High Riggs and then crossing over to the lane down to the hamlet of Stean and back to the car park.

Scar House and Angram reservoirs are best approached on foot along the lane from Middlesmoor which climbs In Moor. Return either by lane alongside the river Nidd or the field-path up to Middlesmoor, or alternatively by the shorter route which passes How

M
8m
4h
oo
**

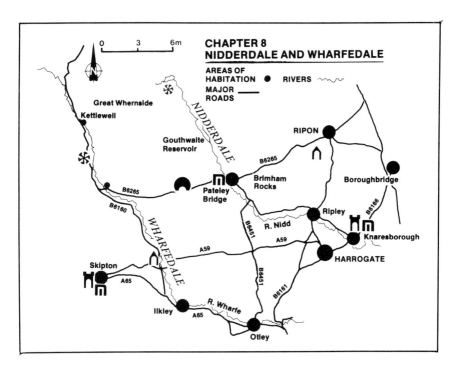

CHAPTER 8
NIDDERDALE AND WHARFEDALE

AREAS OF
HABITATION ●   RIVERS ~~~
MAJOR ___
ROADS

0   3   6m

Great Whernside
Kettlewell

NIDDERDALE

Gouthwaite
Reservoir

RIPON

B6265

WHARFEDALE

Brimham
Rocks

Pateley
Bridge

Boroughbridge

B6265

B6160

Ripley

B6165

R. Nidd

A59   A59   Knaresborough

Skipton

A65   B6451

B6451   B6161   HARROGATE

Ilkley   R. Wharfe

A65

Otley

Gill House and Northside Head.

Down the valley, Ramsgill at the northern end of Gouthwaite Reservoir has a church which was once an outlying chapel of Byland Abbey where the heathen dale dwellers of early times were converted to Christianity.

After the Ice Age, debris left by the retreating glaciers in Nidderdale blocked the flow of the river and for a time there was a natural lake until erosion released its waters. When Bradford Corporation decided to build Gouthwaite reservoir the story was brought full circle with the second flooding of what should rightly be Gouthwaite lake. Not only does the water add to the attractive scenery of the dale, but wild birds and waterfowl have colonised the shores and the area has been designated a Nature Reserve.

When the reservoirs in Upper Nidderdale were being built, access to the site was difficult along the narrow winding lanes of the dale, so a light railway was laid out as far as the dale head to help ease the movement of stores and building materials. When the reservoirs were completed, the line was operated by Bradford Corporation as the Nidd Valley Light Railway carrying goods and passengers. Regretfully, this only recorded instance of a municipally-run railway, was closed in 1929 and the line dismantled in 1936. With the rise of popularity of steam railways what a wonderful attraction this would be if it was still running today.

The moors on either side of Nidderdale are mostly privately owned with very restricted public access. There is, however, the excellent ancient high level way which climbs out of the dale above the top reservoirs and crosses the northern flank of Great Whernside

before descending to Starbotton in Wharfedale. Plenty of valley tracks and paths provide ample walking and one, in particular, which is especially attractive. It starts at Gouthwaite Reservoir by its dam. A footpath descends the dam side to follow the river as far as Pateley Bridge and onwards to Glasshouses. Cross over to the other side of the river to join a path and lane which go as far as Dacre Banks. An infrequent bus service runs up the dale as far as Middlesmoor and with careful timing can be used for the return journey.

L
3½
2h
oo
**

Pateley Bridge occupies a sheltered situation facing south west, which makes it an ideal suntrap, so it is small wonder that it has become such a popular spot for caravanners and picnicers. It is also an ideally convenient centre for the south east dales. There is a signpost marked 'Panorama Walk' in Pateley Bridge; follow it uphill above the town to link up with an easy and level path which commands the extensive view of Nidderdale and the moors beyond. Lead ore was mined in the dale, mostly around Greenhow Hill on the B6265 road where the nine-mile-long Bycliffe vein was worked. Smelting was carried out on the opposite side of the dale below Brimham Rocks at a place now recognised only by the name of Smelthouses.

M
2m
1h
ooc
*

The busy but pleasant B6265 was built as a turnpike road between Knaresborough and Grassington to help move fuel and stores in and lead out of the area. In 1858 a party of lead miners discovered a natural cavern which has since been developed as the show cave known as the Stump Cross Caverns. The system is over 3¾ miles long, but only the show cave is open to the public. This is floodlit to show the

marvellous formations of stalagmites and stalactites and other rock formations.

Back across the dale beyond Pateley Bridge and a little to the south east of the B6265 are the rock formations of Brimham Rocks. These are a series of peculiarly shaped Millstone Grit rocks sculptured into fantastic shapes by the erosion of softer layers topped by others which can withstand the weather more readily. Most have names, some are fanciful but others are more easily identifiable, such as the 'Dancing Bear' and the precariously perched 'Idol' which, although weighing several tons, is perched on a pedestal about a foot in diameter. The best way to see Brimham Rocks is on foot after parking in one of the well placed car parks (SE 209644) off the road between the B6265 and Summer Bridge. The National Trust which owns the area, have erected large scale maps showing the positions and names of the various rocks and the best way is to follow their suggested itinerary and walk it in a clockwise direction. There is an information centre at Brimham House in the centre of the rocks and refreshment hut nearby.

Ripley is an ancient village and was mentioned in the Domesday Book. Fortunately it is now spared the heavy traffic on the A61 since a by-pass was built. Oliver Cromwell stayed here after the battle of Marston Moor, but the village we see today has a French look about it, and no wonder, for it was modelled on one in Alsace-Lorraine for Sir William Amcotts Ingilby in 1827. The French similarity is complete right down to the Hotel de Ville, or town hall, which was added

The Dancing Bear, Brimham Rocks

Ripley Castle

in 1854. The money to rebuild the village was raised from the sale of an outlying farm on which now stands most of the centre of Harrogate.

The Ingilby family have been associated with Ripley since the fourteenth century. Their home, Ripley Castle, is open to the public and is at the lower end of the village beyond the fourteenth-century church with its 'Weeping Cross'. Apparently the name comes from the action of penitents who confessed their sins at its base.

The spa town of Harrogate flourished until the nineteenth century and then fell into a decline after World War I before adopting its present role as a dormitory to the commercial cities of Yorkshire, as well as developing its own identity and modern character. Remnants of the spa still can be seen, in places such as the Opera House and Royal Baths. The Royal Pump Room with the Sulphur Well has been preserved as a museum of life in a spa as it once was. A legacy of the more gentle days of Harrogate lies in the number of parks and open spaces such as the Stray, a two-hundred-acre open space jealously preserved by the inhabitants of the town. On its western edge are the famous Harlow Carr Gardens, owned by the Northern Horticultural Society where there are beautiful displays of flowers throughout most of the year. Harlow Carr also has a more serious purpose being used as a trial ground for new fruit and vegetable plants.

To the north east is the much more ancient town of Knaresborough. The Romans are thought to have built a fort here, but it grew in Anglo Saxon times with the development of a castle to protect against Viking raids. The ruins we see today are a twelfth-century castle left more or less as it was after Cromwell had it made useless during the Civil War. Knaresborough has many interesting buildings and features, such as the oldest chemist's shop in England, along with

Places of Interest Around Pateley Bridge

How Stean Gorge
10 miles north west of Pateley Bridge on the Nidderdale road
Narrow gorge with public access by a series of footbridges. Children's play area, car park. Open all the year.

Gouthwaite Reservoir Nature Reserve
4 miles north west of Pateley Bridge on the Nidderdale road
Reservoir and bird sanctuary and wild fowl, etc. View from road side.

Stump Cross Caverns
5 miles west of Pateley Bridge on B6265
Show caves open to the public, access from road, car parking. Visitor centre, café, gift shop.

Brimham Rocks
2½ miles south east of Pateley Bridge
Natural rock sculptures. National Trust land. Guide leaflet and information available at Brimham House in the centre of the land form. Refreshments. Car parking on perimeter, but access to spectacular rock formations on foot only, 500yds.

the Old Court House Museum and a house carved out of the solid rock overlooking the Nidd. Mother Shipton who in the sixteenth century prophesied the coming of aeroplanes, iron ships, motor cars and men walking under water and many other inventions and events such as world wars, was born in a cave near the Dropping Well on the banks of the Nidd. In the Dropping Well inanimate articles are coated with limestone from lime-laden water dropping from the roof of the crag above and appear to have been turned to stone. Rowing boats can be hired to enjoy the tranquil stretch of the Nidd beneath the shadow of Knaresborough Castle, or for the less energetic a simple stroll by the river completes the pleasures of Nidderdale.

The A59 Harrogate to Skipton road crosses the short Washburn Dale, mostly now flooded to provide drinking water for Leeds and Bradford and with the quaintly named Blubberhouses as its only village.

River Nidd at Knaresborough

Knaresborough Castle

Wharfedale

Glacial action of the ice ages has carved a deep gorge through the easily worn limestone for the river Wharfe. The river left to its own devices prefers a less energetic life and meanders gently along its river plan in the dale bottom for most of the year. This gentleness is something of a sham for in spate after rapidly melting snow or a cloudburst, the Wharfe can become a wild and dangerous river.

The long-distance Dales Way Footpath follows Wharfedale for a good third of its length. The route starts at Ilkley and follows the dale all the way up through Grassington, Kettlewell and Buckden before meeting the Pennine Way for a short distance above Ribblehead. After a sharp dog-leg on Cam Fell the path continues up through Dent and Sedbergh to the Lune Valley and across the M6 by the Crook of Lune. The last lap is through the Lakeland foothills around the Kent and finally down to Bowness on Windermere. As a walk it does not have half the rigours of the Pennine - Way and its length of 73 miles is often scoffed by long-distance walkers, but for scenery there can be no finer walk especially if taken in short easy stages. It can be easily split up over many separate days or taken over a short holiday week. Time on a walk like this should be of no consequence. Apart from the 15 miles from Sedbergh to Burnside accommodation and refreshment stops are relatively easy to find and should not cause problems to anyone who prefers to walk without too many prior arrangements and bookings.

The River Wharfe starts its life at Langstrothdale high up on the moors of Cam Pasture and shares its birthplace with the Ribble, quickly flowing

Wharfedale

down the valley past settlements which within the memory of men not long dead were still used as summer farms in the Scandinavian method of farming. The river flows down past Deepdale to Hubberholme, named after the Hubba who was a Viking chief. Hubberholme is one of those tiny places often ignored, but with its unique appeal, in this case the beautiful Norman church with its rare medieval rood loft painted in red, black and gold. Other woodwork is mostly modern and is the work of Robert Thompson of Kilburn whose trade mark is the carved mouse which you will find hidden in out-of-the-way corners. The 'George' across the road was once owned by the church and every New Year's day the vicar would officiate over a kind of parliament when the 'Poor Pasture' was let for the benefit of the local poor. This custom still operates, but is in the hands of a local auctioneer.

The river at this point makes a sharp turn southwards and the widening valley bottom gives a sheltered site for the first of Wharfedale's picture postcard villages, Buckden. Like most of the dales villages, Buckden was settled by the Norsemen, but they only developed a more sophisticated husbandry on the land already partly settled by earlier man.

On the opposite side of the valley from Buckden an easy path provides a riverside walk to Starbotton or beyond to Kettlewell. The Parklink-Wharfedale bus runs as far as Buckden and can be used for the return journey. That intrepid seventeenth century traveller, Lady Anne Clifford came this way on her journey of inspection to her northern estates. She climbed from Buckden across Buckden Raikes going steeply above the village and then across Stake Moss to Bainbridge. She, not unnaturally, felt that this was one of the most dangerous places she had ever visited. Today the B6160 in summer offers no such terrors.

Starbotton was developed by the Angles but grew with the discovery of lead on Cam Head Moor above a curious ditch built in prehistoric times as some kind of boundary. In 1686 the worst recorded flood in Wharfedale's history wiped out practically the whole village. Only a handful of houses from before this date are still standing.

L
5m
2½h
oooo
*

Places of Interest Around Wharfedale

Kilsey Crag
On B6160, 15 miles north west of Ilkley

Bolton Abbey
A dramatic overhanging limestone crag.

Dales Centre Grassington.
Interpretation centre with guided walks, etc.

Upper Wharfedale Museum
Grassington, on B6160, 8 miles north west of Bolton Abbey
Farming and industrial life of Upper Wharfedale, located in two delightful old cottages.

Grass Wood Nature Reserve
B6160 near Grassington
Ash woodland on limestone habitat.

Barden Tower
On B6160, 4 miles north west of Bolton Abbey
An impressive ruin, one time property of Lady Anne Clifford. Open to the public. Artist's study open, art courses held.

The Strid and Bolton Abbey Woods
Access from B6160
Deep narrow gorge with water worn formations. Nature trails. Fishing, refreshments and car park.

Bolton Abbey
A69, 6½ miles east of Skipton
Ruin of Augustinian Priory. Open to the public.

Ilkley
Art Gallery, Museum and Information Centre.

White Wells Ilkley Moor
Eighteenth-century bath house, now contains display of natural history and geology.

There is a short but steep climb on to the fells above Starbotton. The climb will reward even the most breathless walker, with a view down Wharfedale which will make the effort seem little. The path follows a route straight up Cam Gill Beck across the curiously named Knuckle Bone Pasture to Starbotton Fell. Here the track divides, and one must follow the right hand path over Starbotton Out Moor to join the walled access lane from Cam Head Beck back to Starbotton.

H
3½
2h
oo
**

The road from Wharfedale to Coverdale which starts in Kettlewell is often used to test the climbing ability of cars up the notorious Park Rash, parts of which have a gradient of 1 in 4. For a short while it was on a coach route between London and Richmond via Skipton, but was found to be so difficult that it was soon abandoned. The valley road skirts the edge of Kettlewell and crosses the Wharfe by a lovely old bridge where the masons who built it left a wealth of their coded marks. Kettlewell is Norse for 'bubbling spring'.

Kettlewell is a handy base for a weekend's exploration along a whole series of footpaths and tracks radiating from either side of the village. Some were old routes to other villages, or gave access to high pasture. Others which appear to end abruptly, were sledge roads used for bringing peat down from the high tops in the days when this valuable and easily accessible fuel was used extensively.

A walk in clear conditions and even then to be only undertaken by skilled fell-walkers is the crossing of Great Whernside. By far the easiest approach is by the path which starts on the ancient earthwork at the top of Park Rash. Follow this path until it crosses the north-east ridge of Great Whern-

H
10½
5½
ooo
***

side and turn right to climb over Nidd Head to the summit, then carry on due south for three miles across Conistone Moor and gradually swing to the right to join a path which cuts diagonally down towards Kettlewell.

The long moorland ridge of Old Cote Moor opposite Kettlewell divides Wharfedale from its tributary Littondale where the river Skirfare drains the northern slopes of Fountains Fell and Penyghent. Although very similar in character to the main dale, Littondale is almost a hidden gem with the main village of Arncliffe and its satellites Hawkswick, Litton and Halton Gill. The valley road continues with a struggle over the steep sides of Penyghent to Settle and a branch road from Arncliffe provides an even greater challenge of steep switchbacks below Fountains Fell before timid motorists can thankfully arrive in Malham and safety.

H
12m
6h
oooo

Packhorse trains once used the green lane from Halton Gill to Ribblesdale, but now it makes a quiet way on to Penyghent. Follow this track through Foxup round the northern face of Penyghent passing the deep hole of Hull Pot on the right. Soon the walled Horton Scar Lane is reached by a shooting cabin. Turn left at the hut to follow a well defined path climbing steadily past Hunt Pot to the outlying crags visible on the 2,000ft contour line. An easy track inclines to the right as far as the summit of Penyghent. On the return a short cut can be made below the crags by following the Three Peaks Walk path, down to the green lane where a right turn retraces the route back to Foxup and the tiny hamlets of Halton Gill and Litton which are pretty clusters of old dwellings. The seventeenth century church in Halton Gill is combined with a schoolhouse.

The concave eastern slopes of Fountains Fell dominate Litton. Once this was part of the lands of Fountains Abbey, and it marked the western boundary of their wealth-generating sheep walk. Coal was mined on the summit from shallow bell shaped pits. They can still be traced and near the summit is the sturdy stone structure which was used as a coke-oven.

Arncliffe is mostly built around its attractive village green. The church was first built in the twelfth century, although the building we now see has stood since 1796. The names of Littondale men who fought the Scots at Flodden Field in 1513 are recorded inside the church. Names on the list will still bring a response from their descendants who live in the dale.

Walkers can enjoy the beauty of Littondale and its river by following the path from Litton as far as Arncliffe and then on to Hawkswick on the south bank. Paths link Halton Gill with Hubberholme, Litton with Buckden and Arncliffe with Starbotton. A combination of any two can be used to make a really good round trip walk between the dales. Hawkswick, the lowest village of Littondale, can claim to have been occupied by man since at least the Iron Age. A number of their sites have been found around the village and Douky Bottom Cave high to the south west was inhabited until the fourth century.

Motorists travelling down Wharfedale from its junction with Littondale soon see the remarkable 170ft high Kilnsey Crag with its 40ft overhang. Its receding lower part was carved by glacial action during the last Ice Age. It overshadows the annual Kilnsey Show at the end of August. Kilnsey, once owned by Fountains Abbey

Kilnsey Crag in spring

had a grange here, and has seen busier times, there were once corn and textile mills. Now, limestone is quarried behind the crag, and a trout-farm has been established down the road. Kilnsey is at the eastern end of Mastiles Lane, a green road over to Malham, fortunately still resisting proposals to upgrade it to a motor road, which makes an excellent all-weather footpath.

Across the dale is Conistone, which can trace its history back to Saxon times. Behind the village is the narrow and impressive limestone gorge of Gurling Trough. A path winds its way up the gorge to where it divides. The left-hand fork leads to a lane coming down from the moors, a left turn along this will take the walker back to Conistone. The large area of woodland south of Conistone is all that remains of the forest which once filled Wharfedale. Grass Wood together with the

adjacent Bastow Wood is a Nature Reserve. Both woods are popular attractions and it is possible to follow a path through Bastow and return along another path through Grass Wood.

Man's exploitation of the fells on either side of Grassington had its greatest impact west of the B6160 and B6265 roads where huge limestone quarries deface the landscape. On the scarred fells to the north-east all is now silent, but lead was mined in quantity beneath Grassington Moor until the late nineteenth century. Levels were driven for great distances beneath the moor, the last of which attempted to link the Pateley Bridge workings to those above Grassington and was about 2,610yd long. The remains of the crushing plant can still be seen on Grassington Moor and are accessible on foot from the end of the road past Spring House Farm. Water to drive the plant was scarce and a network of channels can be identified

M
1½m
1h
ooo
*

112

across the hillside to bring water over six miles from a series of small reservoirs. There is also a remarkable complex of smelt-mill flues crossing the moor just below the surface, with a restored terminal stack at the north end.

Grassington is mostly Georgian in appearance and character although its foundations are considerably older and it grew with the fortunes of nearby lead mining. Amongst its old houses is the Fruit Shop which once housed the notorious Tom Lee who murdered a local doctor and threw the body into the Wharfe. Lee was caught and hanged at York in 1766 and his body afterwards was left on a gibbet. Sudden and horrible death features prominently in Grassington's history: it suffered during the Scottish raids of the fourteenth century and worse by far was the visitation by the Black Death in 1349 which killed a quarter of its inhabitants. The Upper Wharfedale Museum of farming and industry together with a fine collection of local minerals is housed in the square.

Although smaller than its neighbour across the valley, Linton has the major church of the area. Built in the fourteenth century it serves the communities of Threshfield, Hebden and Grassington. Linton marks the eastern boundary of the Craven district and certainly the character is Craven, with none of the mountainous feel of the dales, but here a pastoral calm becomes evident with the widening of Craven's broad acres. Linton village, some distance from the church, has a clear stream, a tree-lined green, a Vanbrughian hosptial (almshouse), and fine houses and cottages of the seventeenth and eighteenth centuries. Footpaths on either bank of the Wharfe above and below Grassington

can be linked to give two or three hours pleasant stroll. Above is Ghaistrill's Strid not quite as dramatic as the one in Bolton Woods downstream, but pretty enough to provide a quiet picnic spot.

The glory of Burnsall lies in its riverside position and the attractive bridge completes the picture. Built in 1612, it is still strong enough to stand the frequent batterings of the Wharfe when in spate. Until it was built many bridges had failed this test. The present one is the gift of a local boy who made good and became, like Dick Whittington, a Lord Mayor of London. Burnsall is famous for its Feast Sports which are held on the complicated calendar formulation of the first Saturday after the first Sunday after 12 August. Burnsall's primary school was once an endowed Grammar School and was built in 1610. Adjoining it is a church with Anglo-Danish crosses and tombs and a Norse font, outside are also the combined lychgate and village stocks.

Above Appletreewick and in the deeply carved gorge of Trollers Gill which has an eerie echo, is Parcevall Hall, a beautiful Elizabethan house which once sheltered a notorious highwayman by the name of William Nevison who terrorised travellers on nearby roads. The house is now used as a diocesan retreat and a conference centre. Appletreewick itself has several fine houses at least four to five hundred years old, noteable are High Hall, Monks Hall and Low Hall. The village was once classed as a township and gained a charter in 1311 to hold a fair which became known as the 'Onion Fair'.

The Dales Way follows the river all the way to Bolton Abbey from Grassington and by using the Parklink-

Wharfedale bus a full day can be spent walking along what is undoubtedly the finest stretch of the Wharfe.

Access is permitted to Barden Fell and Barden Moor outside the grouse-shooting season and advantage can be taken of this privilege by using the access point above Howgill village to get on to Barden Fell. No dogs are allowed. The path climbs steeply above the camp site and through Lower Fell Plantation aiming always towards Truckle Crags. A right turn here follows a path through the Valley of Desolation to join the Wharfe below the Strid. The river is followed upstream all the way back to Howgill.

Lady Anne Clifford lived most of her younger days at Barden Tower, which, like most of her other properties, was damaged in the Civil War. She was a remarkable lady, for not only did she devote her energies to building and rebuilding but she also did a tremendous amount of philanthropic work in the area.

Good works featured not only in Lady Anne Clifford's life, as she obviously followed her mother's

Barden Tower

example, who built a hospital at Beamsley in 1593. The building is away from the village by the A59 and can be recognised by an archway which leads into a garden where there is now only a circular building remaining.

The moors west of Barden are also accessible. Two reservoirs use the waters of Barden Beck and the access road up to them from Barden Scales makes a pleasant excursion. Follow the track as far as the upper reservoir and then turn left across the dam to join the bridle way from Rylstone. Turn left along this track and follow it until it joins the Embsay to Barden road. A left turn along this road leads back down to Barden.

Below Barden the Wharfe flows through a cleft known as the Strid. This deep narrow channel has been worn down through softer rock by water action which has also left strange formations and basins. The Strid means 'stride' but only the foolish attempt to jump the gap. Strategically placed lifebelts should be enough warning, but the Strid has claimed many lives of those who did not heed sensible advice.

The Strid

Places of Interest Around Knaresborough

Ripley
On A61, 3½ miles north of Harrogate Attractive 'squire's' village with architectural curiosities. Fourteenth-century castle open to the public.

Knaresborough
Old Court House
Fourteenth-century building, now housing a reconstructed court room scene of 1602.

'House in the Rock'
Eighteenth-century house carved from solid rock overlooking the River Nidd.

Mother Shipton's Cave
Reputed home of a fifteenth-century witch who prophesied many modern inventions.

Dropping Well
Petrifying well alongside Mother Shipton's Cave.

Castle
Norman construction dating from the twelfth century.

Boating
Rowing boats available for hire from the promenade.

Harrogate
Museum, Art Gallery, Harlow Car Gardens. Stray, Rudding Park.

Footpaths follow both banks of the Wharfe into Bolton Woods. Those on the west bank were established between 1789 and 1843 by the vicar of Bolton Priory church, the Reverend William Carr. He began a tradition of public access which has continued up to the present time. The first visitors came from the mill towns of the West Riding by train to the now closed Bolton Abbey station and then by wagonette to the Priory and Strid Woods. For people who normally worked a 50 to 60 hour week this place would be like heaven. The woods are part of the Chatsworth Estates and a small charge is made towards the upkeep of the paths. This is payable at the Strid entrance and the Cavendish Pavilion at the lower end of the woods. Five nature trails are laid out through the woods and an explanatory booklet is on sale.

The soaring ruined arch of Bolton Abbey's east window is the result of the Dissolution by Henry VIII in 1539. Until then it had been home for a small community of Augustinian canons since 1154. Strictly it is not an abbey but a priory, however Bolton Abbey is the most commonly used title and has also been given to the nearby village. The nave was spared during the Dissolution and now acts as the parish church.

Ilkley, the start of the Dales Way, was *Olicana* to the Romans who built a fort here, but little remains except that the site is known. The Old Manor House, now a museum, is built on the

115

Bolton Abbey

Leeds and Bradford. With its back to Rombald's Moor, known throughout the country as Ilkley Moor, setting of Yorkshire's 'national anthem' — *On Ilkla Moor Baht'at* — Ilkley is a fine place to live. Few towns of its size can boast so much open country opening from the top of their High Street.

Visitors to Ilkley can hardly avoid seeing the distinctive mass of the Cow and Calf rocks. Behind them the moor is rich in the carved stones of our prehistoric ancestors who have left not only their cairns and circles but enigmatically carved 'cup-and-ring' and 'swastika' stones. Below the outcrop of Ilkley Crags a solitary building marks the site of 'White Wells' an eighteenth century bath house built by a local benefactor. A walk from the Cow and Calf along the edge of the moor will take in all these features.

The Wharfe continues eastwards away from the dales, but fortunately misses the industrial heartland of Yorkshire. Beyond Ilkley the river passes its sister town of Otley and on round the northern boundary of Yorkshire's major house, Harewood, to skirt the racecourse town of Wetherby and on into the Vale of York, past Samuel Smith's brewery at Tadcaster to join the Ouse and eventually the sea.

site of its west gate. Modern Ilkley developed first with pretentions of being a spa town and later along with neighbouring Otley became a dormitory for the commercial kings of

The Swastika Stone, Ilkley Moor

9 Airedale

On first sight it would seem that the River Aire starts its life as the stream which issues from the letterbox shaped hole at the foot of Malham Cove, for surely it is in a direct line below Malham Tarn, which undoubtedly is the true parent of industrial Yorkshire's major river. Nature however, has other ideas and has arranged for a complicated switch to occur out of sight and below ground. The stream flowing from Malham Tarn disappears undergound at Water Sinks south of the tarn, only to reappear as the quiet spring known as Aire Head about a half mile south of Malham village. The stream issuing from the foot of Malham cove started as an insignificant pair of runnels west of the Littondale road. A waterfall higher than Niagara once flowed over the lip of Malham Cove, but this was before the Aire decided to hide itself away. Local records seem to indicate that the fall dried up some time in the late eighteenth century, although there is

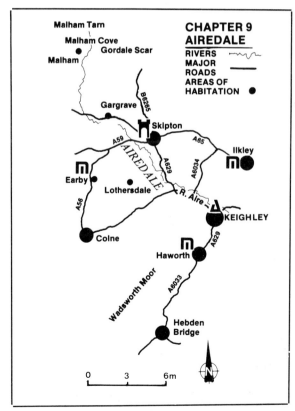

Malham Cove

no factual proof of this.

It is strange to find surface water and especially a lake in limestone country. The reason for it is that patches of Silurian slate, which is impervious to water, occur throughout Craven and the particular patch above Malham holds this tarn.

Beef cattle graze Malham Moor, but it is the sheep which provide the real income to the area. They have been man's mainstay for hundreds of years from the early farmers and later huge flocks roamed the fells and founded the fortunes of Fountains Abbey, which prospered until the Dissolution.

While Fountains Fell is of gritstone and grows a plentiful but sour grass, the land to the east of the upland farm, Tennant Gill, is on limestone and the grass is much shorter, but sweeter. Limestone makes up the whole long complex line of summits running east towards Kilnsey Moor in a maze of outcrops and boulders. This is a fascinating area for the birdwatcher or botanist, and especially the fossil hunter. The land is almost free of visitors so be careful not to break a bone on the often slippery limestone. Paths cross the heights between Malham Moor and Littondale, but none are linked across the tops. However there are few walls and careful navigating in clear weather will provide an entertaining day for either the specialist or purely observant walker.

Malham Tarn and its house are owned by The National Trust and the estate has been devoted to the study of flora and fauna of the area. Malham Tarn House is used as a centre by the Field Studies Council and courses are held there for a variety of student bodies. Once a shooting lodge, the present use for the preservation of wild life has encouraged an increase in the bird population especially the wildfowl which visit the lake during

Places of Interest Around Malham

Malham Cove
$\frac{1}{2}$ mile north of village
Limestone amphitheatre with water-worn pavement on higher level.

Janet's Foss
1 mile east of village
Cascade over a moss-grown tufa block at the bottom of a wooded dell. Nature trail close by.

Gordale Scar
$1\frac{1}{2}$ miles east of village
Deep limestone gorge formed by a collapsed cave system.

Malham Tarn
2 miles north of village
Moorland lake, bird/nature sanctuary. Ideal bird watching area.
Refreshments, car parking and Information Centre available in Malham. For details of a walk which takes in all the main features around Malham see page 120.

their nesting season.

By using two quiet stretches of road round Tarn Moss, and then a footpath, Malham Tarn can be circumnavigated in a couple of hours, but it is a fair bet that the walker's footsteps will be slow along the side of the tarn, especially in spring when the birds congregate and begin their courtship rituals.

Charles Kingsley stayed at Malham Tarn House and was so inspired by the scenery that it became the backcloth for his *Water Babies* novel. He used the magical aspect of the mysterious pool at the foot of Malham Cove as the place where the water babies made their home.

During the formative years of our world, tremendous upheavals took place and today it will be difficult to imagine the cataclysmic earthquakes which rent the face of the earth and reversed the relative heights of land in the Craven area. Nowhere along the Mid Craven Fault is this so evident as at Malham. Land at the foot of Malham Cove started on the same level as the summit of Fountains Fell with the cove marking the fracture line of the fault. On top of Malham Cove is a remarkable limestone pavement, a wide expanse of clefts in the rocks made by the action of water working its way down through weaker sections of this soluble rock. The clefts or 'grikes' are often filled with varieties of ferns such as harts tongue and moonwort. The flat parts between the grikes are known as 'clints'.

In the field below the Cove the ruined walls at right angles to the paths are prehistoric and were built by the first men who settled this sheltered and fertile little valley.

The National Park Authority has provided a large car park and a very useful Information Centre on the edge of Malham village. Malham has attracted visitors for many years. Wordsworth and his sister Dorothy spent some time in the area in 1807 and the line from a sonnet composed after the visit, 'Where young lions crouch' aptly sums up the feel of the crags and precipices of the cove and its neighbours. Malham has many more visitors than it did before the bridge by the green was widened. This was necessary to cope with motors rather than pack horse traffic for which it was first built. Even older than this is Moon Bridge, an ancient clapper bridge a little way upstream by the side of Beck Hall, where on a sunny day the attraction of the river and cream teas can be irresistible. A pack horse road which crossed Malhamdale can still be followed most of its way on footpaths or by a little-used road. This is the route which climbs out from Settle by way of Attermire Scar and crosses Kirkby Fell by Nappa Cross before calling in on Malham. Next it crosses the bridge and climbs across Gordale and steeply up to the moors to join Mastiles Lane and eventually down into Wharfedale by the side of Kilnsey Crag. An alternative and higher route misses Malham by swinging to the left at Nappa Cross and retains its height well above Malham Cove before joining Mastiles Lane near the tarn.

Lead was mined above Malham but the only visible remnant (except for the occasional shaft here and there) is the lonely chimney to the right of the Littondale road which is all that survives of the smelt mill for the area. Mining of a different kind went on below Pikedaw Hill west of Malham where zinc in the form of calamine (zinc carbonate) was extracted from below ground for brass making.

About a mile north-east from Malham on the Bordley road is the breathtaking spectacle of Gordale Scar. Here a collapsed cave system has formed a narrow gorge with towering and overhanging cliffs on either side. Most visitors will not care to emulate the rock gymnasts performing over their heads and in fact most people turn back where the waterfall rushes down its tufa buttress. Tufa is rock which is made from deposits of limestone held in suspension in the stream; as the water flows over the rock it leaves behind minute amounts of lime to form a porous 'reconstituted' stone. Footholds on the buttress to the left of the waterfall make it easier to climb than first impressions might show and in fact the scree slope above is probably more difficult to anyone

wearing footwear other than boots. To the right of the scree slope the river pours through a natural window in the rock wall.

Below Gordale Scar and across the road the river tumbles over another tufa outcrop. This one, known as Janet's Foss, is a perfect gem set amongst shady trees and mossy rocks. Standing by it on a sunny day it is easy to believe the local legend that Janet, a fairy queen, lives behind the outcrop.

There is a walk from Malham which visits all the main features described so far. It starts by the bridge and follows the river downstream for a little way to a gate where a sign-posted path leads to Gordale alongside the stream and into Wedber Wood. Janet's Foss lies at the head of the wood which is set out as a nature trail with plaques explaining the natural features. Above Janet's Foss the path climbs up to and crosses the road before entering the meadow below Gordale Scar. As mentioned earlier the best way up the waterfall is to climb the buttress on the left (when facing); above it a scree slope leads to a field dotted with limestone outcrops and boulders. Pass through this field on a path of springy turf to the road. Turn right along the road and walk to Malham Tarn, but afterwards steps must be retraced until a path is seen diverging on the right. Follow this back to the road where a right-hand turn and then left beyond a gate leads down past Water Sinks (where the Aire disappears underground), and into a dry valley leading to the top of Malham Cove. The way down is to walk (with care) across the limestone pavement to its far end and after crossing a stile on the left follow the zig-zags down into Malham Dale and back to the village.

M
8m
4h
ooo

The Pennine Way which has followed the Aire from Eshton Moor and through Malham village, climbs the Cove, but instead of following the interesting dry valley above it, takes a parallel course along Trougate to the Tarn House. Beyond, the route is semi-artificial, wandering through fields to Tennant Gill and then up to Fountains Fell and across to Penyghent.

M
8m
4h
oo
***

Another walk from Malham, and one less known than that up Gordale starts at Town Head and follows the pack horse way up a narrow lane on to the moors and then heads for Nappa Cross above Pikedaw Hill. A right turn at the cross leads down to the Littondale road. Cross over this road and aim for Low Trenhouse where a right turn will lead you to the dry valley above Malham Cove. Follow the dry dale to the cove and turn either right across the pavement and down the side of the cove or left and climb upwards through a field to join Trougate. Turn right and after a quarter of a mile join the steep road down into Malham.

After the dramatic scenery around Malham the character of Airedale quickly changes to the lush pasture which has made Craven's dairy farms so famous. On either side of the river are two ancient villages. Hanlith to the east was founded by the Angles, and its hall built in 1668 retains a Jacobean flavour despite later alterations. Westwards is the upper valley's main village, Kirkby Malham, where the church was founded in the eighth century. Outside is a preaching cross and a set of stocks which look as though they could be put into use today. Oliver Cromwell is supposed to have witnessed three marriages in the church and there is a signature

which looks like his in the register, but there is nothing else to authenticate his visit to this valley during the long and bitter northern campaign in the Civil War.

The next two villages almost mirror their upstream neighbours in their positions east and west of the river. Calton is on a hilltop to the east and was home for 'Honest' John Lambert, one of Cromwell's officers. Airton is linked more closely to the river, which once powered the former linen mill now converted into flats. Airton was a Quaker stronghold and still holds links with this gentle faith.

Strategically placed in the Aire Gap, Gargrave straddles the A65 as well as the railway and canal. Transport throughout the ages has passed through this village, since prehistoric man used the Aire Gap to cross the Pennines on an established trade route between Ireland and Scandinavia, and the Romans followed suit by building a road from Ribchester to link in with their main north south arteries on either side of York. As the Yorkshire wool trade developed, improvements to the roads between the sheep-rearing areas and the factory towns followed. In 1753 the turnpiking of the Keighley to Kendal road made it much easier for wool to be brought from Westmorland to industrial West Riding. A few years later waterways were promoted which were intended to link Liverpool with the east coast at Hull. In 1770 an Act of Parliament authorised the building of a canal between Liverpool and Leeds and work progressed rapidly on the lower stretches, but it was not until 1790 that the full length was opened, with the completion of the difficult stretch on either side of Gargrave. Canals fell into disuse with the advent of railways for by 1876 the Leeds to Carlisle Railway was in operation.

Today motor traffic speeds through Gargrave on surfaces far smoother than the builders of the turnpike ever envisaged. The railway is still open but is frequently the cause of commercial head-shaking in sections of the British Rail management. The canal, which has not carried any commercial traffic since 1954 has benefited with the increasing popularity of canal cruising. During the holiday season the locks around Gargrave are in almost constant use as pleasure craft climb up to Craven and down to Skipton. So down the centuries Gargrave has in its time seen a great deal of traffic of one kind or another. Traffic has not always been friendly though, the Roman villa south east of the village was found, during recent excavations, to have been sacked in the third century. The Roman villa (SD 939535) is reached along a lane running from the side of the church towards the railway line. The Scots also created much mayhem

Gargrave Locks, Leeds to Liverpool Canal

when they visited Gargrave in 1318 on a cattle raiding excursion.

Footpaths radiate from Gargrave, but perhaps the most interesting walk is one linking the canal and Roman villa. This walk starts by the lock adjacent to the Malham road. Follow the canal towpath 'upstream' as far as East Marton where refreshments can be found. Return by following the Pennine Way route across a series of fields into Gargrave. Turn right at the church to visit the Roman villa about a half mile away, it will be necessary to return by the same lane back into Gargrave to complete this walk.

Side valleys in the dales often lead to pleasant surprises for those who try to avoid the more crowded places. When, as often happens, Malham is overcrowded and the traffic crawls through Skipton, the little Winterburn valley above Gargrave will provide a haven of peace and quiet. Few roads and pathways traverse this valley but those that do are worth following. No villages occupy the main valley but its tributary gives anchorage to three which are very close together. Cracoe is the first, mostly industrialised and

L
9m
4½ŀ
ooo
**

Places of Interest Around Skipton

Skipton
Castle
Eleventh century, restored by Lady Anne Clifford in 1657 and still in excellent repair. Open to the public.

Craven Museum
Situated in the Market Street close to the castle, exhibiting a collection of Craven mementoes. Open most afternoons.

High Corn Mill, Mill Bridge
Still producing corn using the power of two waterwheels. Open to the public.

Leeds and Liverpool Canal
Open to pleasure craft. Boat hire from Gargrave and Skipton. Busy set of locks near Malham road in Gargrave.

Yorkshire Dales Railway
Embsay, 1½ miles north east of Skipton Length of track and a good collection of steam locomotives. Regular steam days.

Earby Museum of Mines
Earby A56, 6 miles south west of Skipton
Largest collection of Yorkshire Dales mining equipment, working models, mineral samples etc. Limited opening.

providing homes for quarry workers and lorry drivers, but Hetton and Rylstone are more attractive places. Rylstone Fell to the east provides some excellent walking and good rock climbing on the gritstone edge of the moor.

The low, elongated hummocky hills on either side of the Leeds-Liverpool Canal below Gargrave are made up of boulder clay left behind by retreating glaciers after they breached the Aire Gap during the last Ice Age.

Craven is roughly shaped like an inverted 'V' with agriculture gradually giving way to industry the closer one gets to Lancashire, but even so there is still much delightful and unspoilt countryside to find. East of Thornton-in-Craven the gentle heights of Pinhaw Beacon (SD 944472) and neighbouring Kelbrook Moor are a blaze of purple heather in August and September during the grouse shooting season. Heather, being the staple diet of grouse, is encouraged, and so we get the side benefit of such a wealth of rich colour in late summer.

Earby never quite succumbed to the growth of its industry as did the other cotton towns further south beneath Pendle. Elizabethan stone houses still can be found in odd corners, often alongside modern factories. One such house has been preserved for use as a lead-mining museum by the Earby Mines Research Group in the seventeenth century grammar school. The collection of mining mementoes ranges from clogs and miner's hats, to working models and a unique ore crusher from Providence Mine near Kettlewell. As it is run by a voluntary society the museum opening times are restricted to Thursday evenings and Sunday afternoons.

On the edge of Lancashire's cotton domain and a mile or two outside Colne, is the unique living museum of Wycoller, a village which started life over eleven centuries ago as a hill settlement, and then in the eighteenth and nineteenth centuries enjoyed a mini-boom as an industrial hamlet. This boom was short lived, as it was based on handloom weaving, and with the advent of mechanical power industry moved to the more open spaces of Colne and the Calder Valley. Wycoller Hall was used by Charlottte Bronte as Ferndean Manor in her novel *Jane Eyre*. Slowly the hall and village fell into decay until 1950, when the Friends of Wycoller came into existence and the decay was halted, but it took until 1973 really to bring about any true preservation when the area was designated a Country Park and Conservation Area. Apart from providing a small visitor information service and generally tidying up the ruins and paths the authorities have had the foresight to leave Wycoller for the visitor to explore and find all its many delightful facets. Car parking is kept outside the village and one must walk in to enjoy the area. Several paths follow the valley as far as the Haworth road and there are numerous permutations on a theme to provide round trips for walkers.

Moving back into Yorkshire along the A6068 towards Airedale, the industrial township of Cowling and its satellite Ickornshaw hold a tenacious foothold in the industrial twentieth century. The moors south of the road are sour and with little interest, but Earl Crag is worth visiting if only to view the curious towers known respectively as Wainman's Pinnacle and Lund's Tower.

Sheltering beneath the bulk of Elslack Moor is Lothersdale, a village of quaint and interesting houses, which has managed the almost impossible task of remaining relatively prosperous without losing any of its character. The woollen mill provides work for most of the inhabants of Lothersdale, and still retains its waterwheel although power is now from the more modern and reliable source of electricity.

The most southerly of Yorkshire's lead mining area and by chance the last to be developed, is between Lothersdale and Cononley. Here a single but rich vein occurs beneath a gritstone layer. While lead had been mined for centuries around this district it was not until 1830 that serious development took place and produced some 150,000 tons of ore in the period up to 1876. The engine house and smelt mill chimney are still in very good condition and have been preserved in a joint venture by the Earby Mines Research Group and the Crosshills Naturalist Society.

Dales and industry both meet and co-exist in Skipton, where miles of sewing cotton are produced. The dales farmer and his wife come down to market to shop alongside visitors out for the day from nearby towns and cities. Good wholesome food is traditionally offered from the many inns

Packhorse Bridge, Wycoller

Old mine workings, Cononley

lining, or not far from, the High Street. Skipton has long been a major market town at the crossroads of routes justifying its claim to be the 'Gateway to the Dales'. Certainly it is ideally situated as a tourist centre. The town was established long before the Normans built a castle here and recorded the name *Sceptone* or Sheeptown. The Domesday Book lists the land around Skipton as Crown land and later it was granted to Robert de Romille.

In 1138 William Fitzduncan, nephew of David, King of Scotland, attacked the castle but was conquered in his turn by Alice de Romille whom he married in 1152. Peace reigned over Skipton for several centuries, during which time the Clifford family took over the castle as protectors against the Scots. In 1642, during the ownership of the indefatigable Lady Anne Clifford, the castle was held by Sir John Mallory and 300 men for three years against Cromwell's troops. Starvation eventually forced their surrender on 21 December 1645. Lady Anne could not return to her castle until 1650 and it took the next 25 years until her death in 1675, to rebuild

it to its present appearance. During this time she undertook the repair of her other properties throughout the north. The imposing gateway to the castle with its Clifford motto *Desormais* (henceforth) is a lasting memorial to Lady Anne's work. The castle is open to the public for most of the year.

An exhibition of old life in Old Craven is on show in the Craven Museum in Skipton Town Hall below the Castle, together with relics of the three-year seige in the Civil War and even older finds. A 'living' museum can be found nearby at High Corn Mill on Ellerbeck where flour is still produced by two waterwheels. The mill is as old as the town, one on the same site having been mentioned in the Domesday Book.

The Springs branch of the Leeds-Liverpool Canal ends in Skipton at a busy basin and its almost constant movement of pleasure craft is only a short distance from the market.

Embsay on the A59, two miles outside Skipton, is the headquarters of the Yorkshire Dales Railway Society who have preserved a section of the old Ilkley to Skipton line. Lack of line has not deterred the society from

Skipton Castle

collecting a large number of locomotives and rolling stock which are
steamed regularly, especially at summer and Bank Holiday weekends.

Skipton has its own 'private' moor
to the east of the town where a
network of paths remain from the
time when people from the remote
farm houses scattered over the moor,
walked to and from Skipton to sell
their produce in the market. A suitable
walk over the moor starts above
Cawder Gill reservoir and aims in a
south easterly direction across the
moor to Vicar's Allotments and then
works its way round to the old farmsteads of High Edge, Haygill Farm
and Snow Hill Top. Continue northwards from here ignoring the farm
lane and follow a path to the left of the
wood ahead. Beyond the wood the old
bridle way from Addingham to Skipton is joined, turn left along this and
back into Skipton.

M
5m
2½h
oo
**

Ever-increasing industrial towns
line the Aire and the clear waters of
Malham Dale are more and more
polluted as the river approaches
Leeds. High up to the east is Rombald's Moor and as we have previously
seen in the chapter on Wharfedale,
even though many tracks cros the
moor from one valley to the other, few
paths actually go round. However it is
possible to walk from Silsden to
Riddlesden on recognised rights of
way. This walk starts in Silsden and
then follows the road steeply up to the
moor by way of Brunthwaite, passing
beneath Brunthwaite Crag to Ghyll
Grange where there is a choice of two
routes, the longest climbs beyond the
grange and swings around the valley
head beneath Rough Holden to join
the shorter route which is the continuation of the farm lane south through
Ghyll Grange. This lane eventually
joins a high level road at Holden Gate.
Turn left at the road and after a few
yards right and down hill to Highwood

M
8n
4h
o
**

Head and zig-zag down through a built-up area to the canal at Leaches Bridge. Turn right along the towpath, passing above Holden Park Golf Course and eventually back into Silsden.

Another walk in the area follows the still unpolluted River Aire. Start from the A629 Skipton road by the river bridge below Kildwick and walk downstream on north bank through water meadows and cross the Silsden road above Steeton. Continue through the fields to Howden House and then by lane to Lower Holden. Turn left on to the canal tow path and follow this all the way through Silsden to Kildwick.

L
10m
5h
oo
***

On no account should Keighley be written off as just another industrial town. Its art gallery in Cliffe Castle is worth visiting, as is its modern town centre, if only to see the neolithic 'cup and ring' stone which was uprooted from its true place on the moors to make an unusual town centre feature. Just outside Keighley on the Bradford road is East Riddlesden Hall, built in 1642, it boasts a magnificent banqueting hall and one of the finest timbered barns in the north of England. The National Trust owns the property, which is open from April to October.

Keighley and Worth Valley Railway

In 1867 a railway line was opened to link the industrial mill towns in the Worth valley to the main line at Keighley. This branch line continued to serve the scattered communities of the valley until 1962 when it was no longer considered an economical proposition. With the nostalgic growth of interest in steam engines it was a heaven sent opportunity for the members of the Keighley and Worth Valley Railway Preservation Society who had banded together for the specific purpose of bringing the line back to life and especially to run it as a commercial venture using steam locomotives. A great deal of work was necessary both to bring the line and rolling stock up to the high standards required by the Ministry of Transport and probably more importantly to raise the necessary cash to fund the venture. Money was needed not only to purchase the line, but also to buy the rights to use Platform Four on Keighley station. At 2.35pm on Saturday 29 June 1968 the hopes and ambitions of all the many people who had worked towards the re-opening of the line were realised, when a beflagged train pulled away from Keighley station drawn by two locomotives. Since then the society has run steam trains every Saturday, Sunday and Bank Holidays and on certain weekdays in summer. The whole venture continues to be operated by enthusiastic volunteers, and all the profits are ploughed back to help buy new rolling stock which is fully preserved and on view in the station yards of Haworth and Oxenhope. Film and TV companies have been quick to realise the scenic potential of the Worth Valley line and have used it many times, the best known being when both the BBC and EMI used it to film sequences of both the TV and screen versions of E. Nesbit's *The Railway Children*.

A trip on the Worth Valley line can be included in a visit to Haworth, if only as a pilgrimage to the parsonage home of the Brontë Sisters, daughters of the Reverend Patrick Brontë who was curate of Haworth's Church of Saint Michael and All Angels. Here is where Anne, Charlotte and Emily wrote their novels, set so often amongst local buildings and places. Without its links with the Brontës, Haworth would still be worth visiting for the atmosphere which recalls the nineteenth century; from its cobbled main street to the gritstone houses laid out in a planners' nightmare and being attractive as a result. One must forgive the slight air of commercialism which has made local traders link the name of Brontë to almost every saleable item, they have a living to make after all.

Penistone Hill above the village has been made into a Country Park and is ideally situated for picnics, or gentle wandering on the edge of the moors. In late summer the sheer enjoyment of the acres of heather recalls the love that the Yorkshire composer Delius had for the rolling moors and open skies of his native county. This is the sunny view of Yorkshire, rather than the sullen impetuousness of the Brontë sisters which is more fitted to a wild stormy day when the dripping clouds cover everything.

A walk that Brontë devotees will follow is the one to Top Withins Farm, or Wuthering Heights. The farm now a ruin, is a typical hill farm made uneconomical when reservoirs were built on good valley-bottom land. Emily enlarged the building in *Wuthering Heights*, but on a wild and

Gordale Scar, Malham

Ilkley Moor

Wycoller

Lothersdale

foggy day late in the year, it is not difficult to people it with the ghosts of Catherine and Heathcliff. The path to Top Withins starts at the cross roads between the Country Park and Lower Laithe Reservoir. Turn left at the cross roads and follow a lane which soon narrows to a path and leads down into the valley, passing on the way a series of small waterfalls and a stone seat, all of which have associations with Emily Brontë. The track climbs up towards the moor where the stark ruin of Top Withins is marked with a plaque indicating its associations.

The Pennine Way route passes Top Withins and two miles further on is Ponden Hall, also with Brontë associations. This house is reputed to be the Thrushcross Grange in *Wuthering Heights*. The building has been preserved with a lot of care and attention given to the spacious rooms, with their massive oak beams and wide stone fireplaces. Pennine Way walkers and seekers of Brontë lore can all enjoy Ponden as its main use today is to provide food and accommodation.

Following the Pennine Way southwards the route crosses the watershed from the Aire into the last of the Northern Pennine valleys, the Calder. Although no longer dales' country and heavily industrialised around the actual river, the Calder Valley offers an amazing variety of lonely moors, deep wooded valleys and unspoilt villages with a heritage which seems to have remained almost unaltered since the eighteenth century. Then industrialisation meant handloom weaving in tiny cottages which are still identifiable by the rows of windows in their attic rooms. A packhorse trail crossed Widdop Moor from Burnley to Halifax and the tiny inn on the Hebden Bridge to Colne road offered them shelter.

Below the Pack Horse Inn, Hebden Water leads down into a lovely wooded valley where Hardcastle Crags have, on occasions, served as the setting for a traditional open air parliament for Swiss nationals living in this country. Hebden Bridge with its terraced cottages appearing to defy gravity makes an ideal centre for Calderdale, or perhaps the visitor will stray to Heptonstall high up on its hillside. Heptonstall, with its Easter Pace Egg play whose traditions are lost in the mist of time, where paganism and Christianity are delightfully intermingled, is one of Yorkshire's most rewarding villages for visitors interested in the domestic weaving trade.

Across the valley is Mankinholes, dominated by the obelisk on Stoodley Pike which was erected to commemorate the defeat of Napoleon in 1814. It has collapsed twice and been restored each time. The tower can be visited by following a flagged path out of Mankinholes to Witherns Gate and then left along the moor edge to Stoodley Pike. From there descend for about a half mile to a cart track, called pretentiously, London Road, and left along it back to Mankinholes.

A long distance path known as the Calderdale Way roughly follows the watershed of all the tributaries of the Calder. It visits many fascinating places and crosses quiet moors and offers fifty miles of interesting walking which can easily be split into seven days splendid walking. Perhaps you may care to try it?

Further Information For Visitors

BUILDINGS AND GARDENS OPEN TO THE PUBLIC

Browsholme Hall
Bashall Eaves, near Clitheroe.
Tel: Stonyhurst 330
Home of the Parker family since 1507.
Tours conducted by member of the family.
Open: Easter, Spring Bank Holiday and
one week either side of Summer Bank
Holiday. Parties of at least four by
appointment from mid-May to end of
September.

Constable Burton Hall
3½ miles of Leyburn on A684.
Georgian Hall. Gardens open to public,
but the hall by appointment only.

Harlow Car Gardens
Harrogate, on south-west edge of town
approached from B6162
Run by the Northern Horticultural Society. The gardens specialise in testing new
varieties of fruits and vegetables as well as
flowers and shrubs. Free coach and car
parks.

Newby Hall
Newby, 4 miles south of Ripon on the
Boroughbridge old road.
Tel: Boroughbridge 2583
Magnificent hall with landscaped gardens.
Built in 1690s, enlarged and redecorated
in 1760s by Robert Adam. Open to the
public during summer months.
Open: Gardens and restaurant, Easter
and April to October 11am-5.30pm, every
day except Monday, but open Bank
Holiday Mondays.
Hall and Train: April to October, every
day except Monday. Also Easter and
Bank Holiday Mondays, 1-5pm, plant
stall, steamboat, children's playground,
steam railway (miniature).

Norton Conyers
Near Wath, 3½ miles north of Ripon.
Fine Jacobean house and garden.
Open: all year, Monday-Friday; April to
October, Saturday and Sunday 2-5.30pm.
Garden centre and refreshments.

Parceval Hall Gardens
Skyreholme, near Appletreewick, 10 miles
north of Ilkley.
Secluded gardens in Trollers Gill.
Open: Easter to October, daily 10am-
4pm.

Stonyhurst College
Hurst Green, near Clitheroe.
Tel: Stonyhurst 345
Catholic Public School founded in 1593,
main building dates from 1377. Open to
visitors by prior appointment.

ABBEYS, CASTLES AND OTHER HISTORIC BUILDINGS

Appleby Castle
Appleby, on the A66 Penrith/Brough
road.
Tel: Appleby 51402
Norman keep set in attractive gardens.
Examples of Roman armour and medieval
furniture. Rare Breeds Survival Trust
Centre.
Open: Easter Friday to Easter Monday
10.30am-5pm; May to September, daily
10.30am-5pm. Special party rates by
arrangement. Free car park. Picnic areas.

Barden Tower
Barden, Wharfedale, on B6160 2¾ miles
north-west of Bolton Abbey.
Tel: (075672) 616
Eleventh-century hunting lodge above the
river Wharfe. Part of the building is still
inhabited and offers accommodation and

refreshments. Artist's studio open daily May to October, by appointment other times. Drawing, painting and etching courses held at certain times.

Barnard Castle (English Heritage)
Barnard Castle, on the A67 in the centre of the town.
An imposing Norman stronghold on the precipitous north bank of the river Tees.
Open: Mid-March to mid-October, (weekdays) 9.30am-6.30pm, (Sunday) 2-6.30pm; October to March (weekdays) 9.30am-4pm, (Sunday) 2-4pm; also Sunday, April to September 9.30am-6.30pm. Charge for admission.

Blanchland Abbey
Blanchland on the B6306, 8 miles south of Hexham.
Remains of this fortified twelfth-century abbey have been incorporated into various buildings within the village. The Lord Crewe Arms incorporates what was once the abbey guest house.

Bolton Abbey
Wharfedale, $6\frac{1}{2}$ miles east of Skipton, approached via A69.
Ruins of Augustinian Priory.
Open to the public at all times.

Bowes Castle (English Heritage)
Bowes on the A66, 4 miles south west of Barnard Castle.
Massive twelfth-century stone keep built on site of Roman fort of *Lavantiae* to command the eastern access to Stainmore.
Open daylight hours. Free admission.

Brough Castle (English Heritage)
Brough, 16 miles north east of M6 junction 38, at the junction of A685 and A666.
Norman keep built on the site of a Roman fort.

Castle Bolton
Wensleydale, $4\frac{1}{2}$ miles north-east of Aysgarth on Reeth road.
Fourteenth-century castle which was besieged by the Parliamentary troops in the Civil War. Habitable rooms now used as a restaurant.
Open: April to October, daily (except Monday) 10am-6pm (open Bank Holidays).

Clitheroe Castle
Clitheroe, Lancashire
Ruins of medieval castle in public gardens. Free access during daylight hours.

Egglestone Abbey (English Heritage)
Approached by Rokeby Park road $1\frac{1}{2}$ miles south-east of Barnard Castle.
Picturesque ruin set on a hill above the south bank of the river Tees. The greater part of the thirteenth/fourteenth-century nave survives.
Open: Mid-March to mid-October, weekdays 9.30am-6.30pm, Sunday 2-6.30pm; October to March, weekdays 9.30am-4pm, Sunday 2-4pm.
Free admission. Guide Book available.

East Riddlesden Hall (National Trust)
On A650, 1 mile south-east of Keighley. Seventeenth-century manor house with banqueting hall with Great Barn.
Tel: Keighley 607075
Open: April to October, Wednesday-Sunday, Bank Holiday Monday (closed Good Friday) 2-6pm; June, July, August 11am-6pm. Educational visits Thursdays and Fridays all season by appointment.

Fountains Abbey and Studley Royal
(National Trust)
3 miles west of Ripon off B6265 to Pateley Bridge.
The largest monastic ruin in Britain; founded by Cistercian monks in 1132; landscape gardens laid out 1720-40 with lake, formal water garden and temples; deer park; St Mary's Church built by William Burges 1871-8; Jacobean Mansion House; small museum.
Open: October to March, daily (except Christmas Eve and Christmas Day) 10am-4pm; April to June and September, daily 10am-7pm; July and August, daily 10am-8pm.

Jervaulx Abbey

On A6108 between Leyburn and Masham. Twelfth-century Cistercian Abbey, almost completely obliterated by Henry VIII, but the ground plan and a number of carved stones still remain. Beautiful setting on the banks of the river Ure.

Knaresborough Castle

Castle Yard
Knaresborough.
Tel: (0423) 503340
Home of Plantagenet Kings, later sacked by Cromwell during the Civil War.
Open: Easter Weekend, Spring Bank Holiday, then from Late Spring Holiday to 30 September.

Marrick Priory

Swaledale, ½ mile south west of Marrick village.
Twelfth-century house for Benedictine Nuns now used as a church. Reached by stone causeway from Marrick village. Tranquil situation on a wooded stretch of the river Swale.
Open daylight hours.

Middleham Castle (English Heritage)

Situated in Middleham on A6108 Leyburn to Ripon road.
Impressive ruin of twelfth-century castle, which once was the home of King Richard III.
Open: Mid-March to mid-October, weekdays 9.30am-6.30pm, Sunday 2-6.30pm; October-March, weekdays 9.30am-4pm, Sunday 2-4pm.

Richmond Castle (English Heritage)

Richmond, North Yorkshire
Massive Norman keep founded in 1071 by Alan Rufus.
Open: Mid-March to mid-October, weekdays 9.30am-6.30pm, Sunday 2-6pm; October to March, weekdays 9.30am-4pm, Sunday 2-4pm.

Ripley Castle

3 miles north of Harrogate on A61.
Tel: (0423) 770157
Present building dates mainly from 1780, but oldest part is fifteenth-century. Home of the Ingilby family. The nearby village has a strong French atmosphere having been built in 1827 modelled on one in Alsace-Lorraine.
Open: Gardens, April to mid-October, daily 11am-5.30pm.
Castle, April to May, Saturday and Sunday 11.30am-4.30pm; June to mid-October, daily (except Monday and Friday) 11.30am-4.30pm; Bank Holidays in season 11am-4.30pm.

Sawley Abbey (English Heritage)

Sawley, on the A59 3¾ miles north-east of Clitheroe.
Ruins of medieval monastery. Free access during daylight hours.

Skipton Castle

Centre of Skipton town.
Eleventh-century castle, restored in 1657 by Lady Anne Clifford. Maintained by local organisation.
Open: all year (except Christmas day and Good Friday) weekdays 10am-dusk, Sunday 2-6pm (or dusk if earlier).

Whalley Abbey

Whalley, on A59 4 miles south of Clitheroe. Elizabethan manor house and ruins of thirteenth-century abbey. Maintained by Blackburn Diocese. Manor house used as a retreat centre. Attractive flower gardens, gift shop and craft centre.
Open: Easter to October, weekdays 11.30am-4.30pm, Sunday 1-4.30pm.

MUSEUMS

===

Beamish North of England Open-Air Museum

Stanley, Co Durham
Off A693 Stanley to Chester-le-Street road.
Tel: Stanley (0207) 231811

A 200 acre open air museum of Northern life, where buildings from the region have been rebuilt and furnished as they once were, with a 1920s Town Street with shops, houses, pub etc.; a northern colliery with mine and pit cottages; a working farm and a NER station and steam locomotives. Working electric trams.
Open: Easter to mid-September, daily 10am-6pm; Mid-September to Easter, daily (except Mondays) 10am-5pm. Last admission always 4pm.

Bedale Hall Museum
Bedale. DL8 1AA
Tel: (0677) 23131
Seventeenth-century hall.
A Georgian Ballroom with fine Italian plaster ceiling and rare scarfe jointed pine floor. Museum displays local art and crafts, tradesman's tools, clocks, coins, weights and many other interesting objects.
Open: May to September, 10am-4pm, or by appointment.

The Bowes Museum
Barnard Castle.
Barnard Castle, 1/2 mile from town centre on Whorlton road.
Tel: Teesdale 37139
A collection of national importance housed in a French-style château. It includes paintings by El Greco and Goya and extensive collections of furniture, pottery, porcelain and tapestries. Administered by Durham County Council.
Open: Weekdays, May to September, weekdays 10am-5.30pm; October, March and April 10am-5pm; November to February, 10am-4pm; Sunday, summer 2-5pm, winter 2-4pm. Closed one week Christmas and 1 January. Charge for admission.

Brontë Parsonage Museum
Haworth
Keighley
Tel: (0535) 42323
Many original manuscripts and personal memorabilia of the Brontë family.

Open: April to September, 11am-5.30pm; October to March 11am-4.30pm; Closed 24, 25, 26 December and for three weeks in February.

Clitheroe Castle Museum
Castle Hill
Clitheroe, Lancs.
Tel: (0200) 24635 or 25111
Small museum devoted to life in the nineteenth century. Museum contains an important collection of carboniferous fossils and a selection of items of local significance.
Open: Easter to October, daily 2-4.30pm and Bank Holidays 11am-4.30pm.

Courthouse Museum
Castle Yard, Knaresborough.
Tel: (0423) 503340
Museum of local history with original Tudor court.
Open: 1 April to 30 September; October to March, Sunday only, 1.30-4.30pm.

Craven Museum
Town Hall, High Street, Skipton.
Tel: (0756) 4079
Collection illustrating history and archaeology of Craven.
Open: April to September, Monday, Wednesday, Thursday and Friday 11am-5pm, Saturday 10am-12noon and 1-5pm, Sunday 2-5pm; October to March, Monday, Wednesday, Thursday and Friday 2-5pm, Saturday 10am-12noon and 1.30-4.30pm, closed Sunday. Closed on Tuesdays all year.

Earby Museum of Mines
School Lane
Earby
On A56, 6 miles south-west of Skipton. A large collection of Yorkshire dales mining equipment, working models and mineral samples. Run by voluntary society. Open: Thursday evenings 6-9pm and Sunday afternoons 2-6pm.

Georgian Theatre Royal and Theatre Museum
Victoria Road, Richmond.
Tel: (0748) 3021
A unique Georgian theatre and adjacent museum which links modern productions with 'the good old days' through hand bills and costumes, etc.
Open: May to September, weekdays 2.30-5pm, Saturday and Bank Holiday Monday 10.30am-1.30pm.

Green Howards Regimental Museum
Trinity Church Square, Richmond.
Tel: (0748) 2133
Memorabilia of this famous Yorkshire Regiment since its formation in 1688.
Open: April to October, weekday 9.30am-4.30pm, Sunday 2-4.30pm; November and March, Monday-Saturday 10am-4.30pm; February,. Monday-Friday 10am-4.30pm. Closed all December and January.

Harrogate Art Gallery
Victoria Avenue, Harrogate.
Tel: (0423) 503340
Permanent collection of many fine oil and water paintings, including paintings by Turner and Constable.

Ilkley Art Gallery and Museum
Ilkley, in centre of town.
Tel: Ilkley 600066
Museum on the site of Roman fort, and many artefacts from this are on display.
Open: daily 10am-6pm. Closed Monday (except Bank Holiday Monday).

Killhope Wheel Lead Mining Centre
2½ miles west of Cowshill on A689 in Upper Weardale.
Tel: Durham 64411 ext. 2354
A restored lead crushing mill, with a 34ft high waterwheel. The area's best-preserved lead mining site. Exhibition about lead mining and life of the miner in one of the restored buildings.
Open: April, May, June and September, daily (except Mondays) 10.30am-5pm; July and August, daily; October weekends and Wednesday; November to end of March by appointment for parties.

Museum of North Craven Life
Victoria Street, Settle.
Tel: Bentham 61163 or Clapham 414.
Display of man in the countryside near Settle since prehistoric times, housed in a seventeenth-century building. Also temporary exhibitions, guide cards, demonstrations and lectures.
Open: May to June, Saturday, Sunday 2-5pm; July to September, daily (except Monday) 2-5pm; October to April, Saturday 2-5pm.

Museum of Steam
On the A682, 2 miles south of Gisburn.
Tel: Gisburn 322
Small collection of steam driven vehicles, including showmen's engines, all steamed during the summer.
Open at all reasonable times. Free. Access for coaches.

Nidderdale Museum
Old Council Offices, Pateley Bridge, Nidderdale.
Recently enlarged with several shop displays, Victorian living room and solicitor's office.
Open: all year, every Sunday; Easter to October, weekends 2-5pm; Whitsun to October, daily.

Old Court House
Adjacent to Knaresborough Castle.
Fourteenth-century building with a reconstructed courtroom scene of 1602 with figures dressed in period costume.

Pig Yard Museum
Castle Hill, Settle.
Exhibitions of items of archaeological interest found locally.
Open by appointment only. Write to the curator.

Richmondshire Museum
Ryders Wynd, Richmond.
Museum of bygone Richmond's County before its amalgamation with Yorkshire.
Open: 21 May to 24 September, daily 2-5pm.

Swaledale Folk Museum

Reeth Green, Reeth, Swaledale.
Tel: Richmond 84373 (evenings only)
A museum of agricultural life and mining in bygone days in this area.
Open: Easter to September, daily 10.30am-6pm.

Upper Dales Folk Museum

Station Yard, Hawes.
Tel: Hawes 494
Exhibition of life on dales farm based on the Marie Hartley and Joan Ingilby collection. Located in the goods shed of the old railway station.
Open: Easter or 1 April to September, Monday-Saturday 11am-1pm and 2-5pm, Sunday 2-5pm; October, Tuesday, Saturday and Sunday only.

Upper Wharfedale Museum

The Square, Grassington.
Tel: Grassington 752800
Displays of dales farming and industry of the past; also included are veterinary equipment and a mineral collection.
Open: April to October, daily 2-4.30pm.

Wakeman's House Museum, Ripon.

One-time home of the Wakeman, a medieval guardian of the town. The custom of blowing the Wakeman's curfew horn is still maintained. House is also an information centre.

White Wells

Ilkley Moor
Display of natural history and geology. Accessible only on foot.
Open: Summer, Saturday, Sunday and Bank Holiday Monday 2-6pm.

The Yorkshire Museum of Carriages and Horsedrawn Vehicles

Aysgarth, Wensleydale, on the A684.
One of the most comprehensive collections in England of horsedrawn vehicles used by the country squire and his estate.

OTHER PLACES OF INTEREST

Alston Market Cross

Alston, on the A686, 19 miles north-east of Penrith.
Covered market stand in main street.

Aysgarth Falls

Aysgarth.
A stepped series of falls for one mile on either side of the Aysgarth to Carperby Road.

Brimham Rocks (National Trust)

Near Pateley Bridge, access from B6265 or B6165.
Moorland area dotted with natural sculptures from weather-worn gritstone. Car park on perimeter. Trails indicated on information boards lead past most of the better formations. Information centre and refreshments at Brimham House.

Buttertubs

On Thwaite to Hawes road, $2\frac{1}{2}$ miles south of Thwaite.
Shallow pot holes easily accessible from roadside. Car park and information panels.

Cauldron Snout Waterfall

Upper Teesdale, below Cow Green Reservoir. Access from Weelhead Syke car park.

Dropping Well

Knaresborough.
Tel: (0423) 862352
Petrifying well adjacent to Mother Shipton's Cave. Objects placed in the well are coated with stone over a period of several months.

Ebbing and Flowing Well

Buck Haw Brow, Settle.
on A65, $1\frac{1}{4}$ miles north-west of Settle. GR803654.

Gaping Gill Hole

3 miles north of Clapham. GR751727.
Impressive pot hole. Local caving club erects a winchborne chair during Spring and August Bank Holiday.

Glens and Waterfalls of Ingleton
Delightful wooded ravines and waterfalls. Small admission charge.

God's Bridge
GR957126. 2¼ miles west of Bowes on A66. Approach ¼ mile south of Pasture End Farm.
Natural limestone bridge spanning river Greta.

Gordale Scar
1¼ miles east of Malham Village. GR 915642.
A deep limestone gorge formed by a collapsed cave system. Popular rock climbing area.

Hardrow Force
GR 868914. Access behind Green Dragon Inn, Hardrow, 1¼ miles north of Hawes. Highest above-ground waterfall in England.

Hawes Ropeworks Town Foot, Hawes.
Tel: Hawes 487
A working ropeworks specialising in animal halters, church bell ropes, bannister and barrier ropes. Free. Shop etc.
Open: Monday-Friday 9am-5.30 pm (closed ½hr lunch), Saturday in most school holidays, 10am-4pm (summer), closed Sunday.

High Corn Mill
Mill Bridge, Skipton.
Tel: Skipton 2883
Corn mill still using the power of two waterwheels.
Open: Wednesday, Saturday and Sunday 2-6pm.

High Force
Upper Teesdale. GR 881284. Access from B6277 High Force Hotel.
Small fee.

House in the Rock
Knaresborough.
Eighteenth-century house carved from solid rock overlooking the river Nidd.
Open to the public during the summer months.

Janet's Foss
1 mile east of Malham village. GR912634. Cascade over a moss covered rock at the bottom of a wooded dell.

Kilnsey Crag
Wharfedale. GR975679. 4½ miles north-west of Grassington on B6160.
Impressive overhanging limestone crag dominating the landscape.

Low Force
Upper Teesdale. GR 904279. On the B6277 1 mile north-west of Newbiggin.

Malham Cove
½ mile north of Malham village. GR 896641.
Natural limestone amphitheatre with waterworn pavement on high level. Remains of ancient field system below. Explanatory notices nearby.

Malham Tarn
A unique moorland lake and bird/nature sanctuary. Residential courses in all aspects of Natural History run by the Field Studies Council at Malham Tarn Field Centre, Settle.

Mother Shipton's Cave
Knaresborough, on south bank of river approached from B6163.
Tel: (0423) 862352
Reputed home of the fifteenth-century witch who prophesied many modern inventions.

Norber Boulders
1¾ miles north-east of Clapham via A65. Slate boulders left by the retreating Ice Age glacier on limestone pedestals.

Ribblehead Viaduct
6 miles north-east of Ingleton near the B6255. GR 760795.

The Shambles
Settle.
Interesting group of old houses and shops on the east side of the market square.

Stainforth Bridge and Force (National Trust)
GR 817672.
Elegant arched packhorse bridge and attractive waterfall nearby.

The Strid
Wharfedale, 2 miles north-west of Bolton Abbey. GR 063565.
Dramatic narrow cleft through which flows the river Wharfe. Many interesting waterworn rocks.
Warning:- Do not attempt to jump across the Strid, the river is very deep and fast.

COUNTRY PARKS AND VISITOR CENTRES

Bowlees Visitor Centre
Bowlees, Upper Teesdale, on B6277, 3 miles north-west of Middleton-in-Teesdale.
Visual display of natural history of Upper Teesdale. Attractively laid out museum in converted chapel. Picnic site nearby.
Open summer months only.

Cove Centre
Malham
Tel: (07293) 432
Craft workshops, café.

The Dales Centre
Grassington, near Skipton.
Tel: (0756) 752312
Holiday accommodation. Small groups are led by an expert guide to discover the delights of the dales and fells around Grassington. Slide shows and other events organised in the evenings.

Kilnsey Park
Kilnsey, near Skipton
Tel: (0756) 752150
Trout hatchery, picnic site, freshwater aquarium, fishing.
Open: All year, daily 9.30am-5pm.

Slurring Rocks Country Park
Hardcastle Crags, Hebden Bridge. GR 988291.
Attractive wooded valley and gritstone gorge. Refreshments nearby.

How Stean Gorge
Near Pateley Bridge, Nidderdale.
Tel: (0423) 75666
Narrow gorge near the head of Nidderdale, skilfully laid out with walks and foot bridges. Children's play area. Car Park. Open all the year.

Lightwater Valley Action Park
3 miles north of Ripon on the A6108.
Tel: (0765) 85321
Miniature railway, visitor farms, adventure playground, old time fair, boating, golf, hellslide. Fruit picking in season. Restaurants and gift shop.
Open: April and May, Easter week, weekends and Bank holidays; June, July and August, daily; September, weekends 10.30am-3.30pm.

Penistone Hill Country Park
Haworth, $\frac{1}{2}$ mile north of village.
Open moorland on edge of village.

Rare Breeds Survival Trust Centre
Appleby Castle, Appleby, on A66 Penrith to Brough road.
Tel: Appleby 51402
Collection of rare breeds of domestic farm animals, water fowl, pheasants, poultry and owls. Beautifully laid out grounds. Free car park. Picnic areas and tea rooms.
Open: Easter Friday-Easter Monday 10.30am-5pm; May to end September, daily 10.30am-5pm. Special party rates by arrangement.

Whernside Cave and Fell Centre
Yorkshire Dales National Park, Dent, Sedbergh, Cumbria, LA10 5RE, $6\frac{1}{2}$ miles south-east of M6, junction 37.
Tel: Dent (05875) 213 and 218
Residential centre offering courses in cave exploration and fell walking.

Whorlton Lido
5 miles south-east of Barnard Castle.
On privately owned picnic site. Has narrow gauge railway on south bank of river Tees.

Wycoller Hall
Off Haworth Road, 3 miles from Colne. Was used by Charlotte Brontë as Ferndean Manor in *Jane Eyre*.

Wycoller Visitor Centre
Off Haworth Road, 3 miles from Colne. Sensitive preservation of an unspoilt hamlet.

Beacon Fell Country Park
GR 568429. 8 miles north of Preston and signposted from Longridge GR 568429. Conifer woods, forest walks, viewpoint, picnic areas, refreshments.
Open all the year.

ARCHAEOLOGICAL SITES

Ilkley Moor
White Wells, GR 109468
Bath-house erected by eighteenth-century philanthropist for the inhabitants of Ilkley.

Tumuli, etc
Ilkley Moor has innumerable prehistoric remains, and a glance at the map will indicate this fact. The most accessible is the Swastika Stone, at GR 095470: an enigmatic carving on a prominent rock.

Twelve Apostles GR 126451
Stone circle approached by path from Whitewells to Baildon.

Kirkland, 'Hanging Walls of Mark Anthony'
9 miles north-west of Appleby, GR 652322. Fine examples of prehistoric cultivation terraces.

Long Meg and Her Daughters
Little Salkeld, 4½ miles north-east of Penrith, GR 571372.
A huge oval stone circle (360 x 298ft), with twenty-seven of a probable sixty stones still standing. Long Meg is the tallest stone, 10ft high, with symbolic cup and ring carvings.

Roman Fort
Bainbridge, Wensleydale, GR 937902.

Fortification visible on prominent mound east of Bainbridge village.

Ribchester Roman Fort
Ribchester on B6245, 4½ miles north of Blackburn.
Only the perimeter wall visible and partially excavated granary remains. Open during daylight hours.

Whitley Castle Roman Fort
B6292, 2½ miles north-west of Alston, GR 695487.
Excellent example of a well fortified Roman Fort. Free access by public footpath from B6292 at Castle Nook Farm.

NATURE RESERVES

Gouthwaite Reservoir Nature Reserve
Nidderdale, 4 miles north-west of Pateley Bridge.
Bird sanctuary not freely accessible to general public, but many birds can be seen from the roads and trackways surrounding the reservoir.

Grass Wood Nature Reserve
Wharfedale, 1½ miles north-west of Grassington.
Ash Woodland on limestone. Owned and maintained by the Yorkshire Wildlife Trust Ltd.
Parties by arrangement only.

Upper Teesdale National Nature Reserve
A botanically unique area of 8,600 acres (3500 hectares). The area around Cauldron Snout is accessible to the general public and a nature trail on Widdybank Fell allows visitors to see some of the rare plants flowering in their season. Field studies are based at Moor House.

NATURE TRAILS

Clapdale Woods (Reginald Farrer Trust)
½ mile north of Clapham. Trail is in memory of Reginal Farrer (1880-1920).

authority and collector of alpine plants. Himalayan shrubs and trees are featured in the trail.

Aysgarth Falls Nature Trail
GR 010887.
Nature trail starts from National Park Information Centre, and follows wooded river bank above a series of attractive waterfalls.

Bolton Abbey Woods and the Strid
Wharfedale, approached from B6160, GR 077553.
Several trails of varying length start and finish at the Cavendish Pavilion. Refreshments available.

Gibson's Cave Nature Trail
Bowlees, Upper Teesdale. Access from B6277, 3 miles north-west of Middleton-in-Teesdale.
Nature Trail starts from Bowlees Visitor Centre car park and picnic area. Interesting short walk through wooded valley.

Hardrow Force
Rear of Green Dragon Inn, Hardrow, near Hawes.
Natural amphitheatre and highest above ground waterfall in England.

Janet's Foss Woods
1 mile east of Malham village, GR 912634.
Trail laid out with explanatory plaques in woodland below Janet's Foss Waterfall.

Sedbergh Town Trail
Short interpretive walk around Sedbergh.

Sedgwick Geological Trail
Lower Garsdale.
Short ($1\frac{1}{2}$ hours approx) trail laid out on Longstone Common, crosses Dent Fault where the complex folds of Lake District rocks meet the horizontally bedded Carboniferous Limestone and Yoredale Shales of the Pennine Dales.
Trail in memory of Adam Sedgwick (1785-1873) father of modern geology.

Spring Wood Nature Trail
Whalley, near Clitheroe, GR 741361
Mixed woodland. Picnic site.

Valley Walks
Ilkley, Wharfedale.
Short waymarked routes from $\frac{1}{2}$ mile to $3\frac{1}{2}$ miles.

Waterfalls Walk
Ingleton
Follows a series of natural waterfalls on the River Greta.

Weelhead Syke Nature Trail
Cow Green (off B6277 Upper Teesdale)
Trail starts from scenic car park above Cow Green Reservoir. Open moorland, semi-alpine and tundra plants.

FISHING

Most rivers with game fish are privately owned and fishing permits can be bought locally. Rod licences are issued by the various water authorities (addresses below), who also allow game and coarse fishing on reservoirs and stretches of river under their control. Each authority publishes a descriptive leaflet.

North-West Water Authority,
Rivers Division,
PO Box 12,
New Town House,
Buttermarket Street,
Warrington WA1 2QG
Tel: (0925) 53999
River Areas: Ribble, Lune and Eden.

Amenity and Recreation Officer,
Yorkshire Water Authority,
Rivers Division,
21 Park Square South,
Leeds
Tel: (0532) 440191
River Areas: Aire, Wharfe, Nidd, Ure, Swale.

Northumbrian Water,
Northumbria House,
Regent Centre,
Gosforth,
Newcastle NE3 3PX
Tel: (0912) 843151
River Areas: Tees, Wear, Derwent, Tyne,
Aln, Coquet, Wansbeck.

Owners of other lakes and mill pools, such
as Malham Tarn and Foster Beck Hemp
Mill near Pateley Bridge, issue day tickets.

The useful Northern Angler's Handbook
covers details of all fishable waters and is
on sale at bookshops and Yorkshire Dales
National Park Information Centres.

BOATING AND SAILING

Knaresborough
Rowing boats available for hire throughout the summer months on the river Nidd.

Leeds and Liverpool Canal
Pleasure boats available for holiday hire
from:

British Waterways,
Bank Newton Lock,
Gargrave
Tel: Gargrave (075678) 428

Yorkshire Dales Hire Cruises,
Bank Newton
Gargrave
Skipton BD23 3NT
Tel: Gargrave (075 678) 492

Snaygill Boats,
Skipton Road,
Bradley,
Skipton
Tel: Skipton 5150

Black Prince Narrowboats Ltd.,
Silsden,
Steeton
Tel: Steeton 53675

Pennine Cruisers,
Coach Street,
Skipton
Tel: Skipton 5478

Semerwater
Countersett, Raydale, 2 miles south-west
of Bainbridge, via A684.
Popular picnic area with unofficial small
craft use.

Derwent Reservoir
Derwentdale.
Club and day sailing. Picnic areas.

GOLF

Golf Courses:	Masham
Whalley	Catterick
Clitheroe	Richmond
Keighley	Bedale
Skipton	Barnard Castle
Settle	Appleby
Harrogate	Allendale
Knaresborough	Alston Moor

SKIING

Winter Ski Slopes
  Upper Teesdale
  Cross Fell
  Allenheads, Allendale
  Westgate, Weardale

Cross Country
  From Dufton Youth Hostel

Indoor Ski Slope
  Catterick

Tours set up by local ski clubs.

ZOOS

Cunningham Hall, Knaresborough
Tel: (0423) 862793
Open all year 10am until dusk.

RIDING AND PONY TREKKING

Caton School of Equitation,
Quernmore Road,
Caton,
Lancaster
Tel: (0524) 770694

Fitton & Son,
Bank Newton,
Gargrave
Tel: Gargrave 243

Kilnsey Trekking Centre,
Grassington
Tel: Grassington 752861

Sinderhope Pony Trekking Centre,
Broadgate,
Sinderhope,
Allenheads
Northumbria NE47 9SH
Tel: (043485) 266

West Park,
Lunedale,
Middleton-in-Teesdale,
Co Durham
Tel: (08334) 380

BIRD WATCHING

Courses in bird watching are organised
by:

Field Studies Council,
The Malham Tarn Field Centre,
Settle,
North Yorkshire BD24 9PU

YHA Adventure Holidays,
Trevelyan House,
8 St Stephen's Hill,
St Albans,
Herts

Bird Guide,
Ashville,
Rose Bank,
Burley-in-Wharfedale,
West Yorkshire

SWIMMING POOLS

Grassington, Upper Wharfedale School
Ingleton (heated open air, summer season)
Settle, next to Settle Middle School
Tel: Settle 3262

Skipton, Aireville Park
Tel: Skipton 2805

Stanhope
Richmond, Old Station Yard
Tel: Richmond 4581

Wolsingham

LONG DISTANCE FOOTPATHS

The Pennine Way
This route starts at Edale in Derbyshire
and finishes at Kirk Yetholm in Scotland,
passing through the area described in this
book.

The Dales Way
A pleasant valley and fell walk, of several
days duration, starts at Ilkley in Wharfedale and finishes at Windermere.

Coast to Coast Walk
From St Bees Head in Cumbria to
Ravenscar on the Yorkshire Coast, coincides
with both the Pennine Way and the Dales
Way above Ribblesdale.

The Calderdale Way
A walk following the approximate bounds
of the Calder Valley watershed, linking
public rights of way and permissive paths.
Can be completed in five easy stages. 50
miles total length.

SPORTS CENTRE

Coulthurst Craven Sports Centre,
Sandylands,
Carleton New Road,
Skipton BD23 2AZ
Tel: (0756) 5181

DALES RAIL

A fully integrated rail and bus service operates on certain dates throughout the summer based on the Leeds to Carlisle line with connections from Preston and Blackburn to Hellifield.

There are organised walks planned each year timed to start and finish with convenient trains and buses, or by careful use of the Dales Rail Time Table more ambitious routes may be planned.

Further details from Yorkshire Dales National Park Committee Information Centres, or from:

Dales Rail,
Yorkshire Dales National Park,
Colvend,
Hebden Road, Grassington BD23 5LB
Tel: (0756) 752748

Friends of Dales Rail,
c/o 3 Rochester Terrace,
Leeds LS6 3DF

British Rail
Skipton
Tel: Skipton 2543

Settle
Tel: Settle 3536

Intermediate stations of Settle-Carlisle Line open for Dales Rail.

CYCLE HIRE

While the Yorkshire Dales offers miles of minor roads ideally suited to cycle touring at all levels, from the quiet family wander to more serious long distance rides, as yet cycles may only be hired from the following points:

Ingleton:
Richard's Cycles,
The Square, Ingleton.
Tel: Ingleton 41094

Settle:
The Cycle Shop,
Duke Street, Settle.
Tel: Settle 2216

Wharfedale:
The Dales Centre,
Tennant Arms,
Kilnsey
Tel: Grassington 752301/752312

Hawes:
Dales Cycle Hire
Tel: Hawes 487

STEAM RAILWAYS

Keighley and Worth Valley Railway
Haworth Station, Haworth, Keighley, W Yorkshire
Tel: (0535) 43629 (talking timetable)
Steam line operated by preservation society between Keighley British Rail Station and Oxenhope near Haworth. Steam trains run every weekend, March to October, Bank holidays and daily July and August.

South Tynedale Railway Preservation Society
Alston, on A686
Tel: (0498) 81696
Narrow gauge railway along part of the old branch line towards Haltwhistle. Trains at weekends Easter to September; daily during summer. Shop, café, tourist information, parking at Alston Station.

Yorkshire Dales Railway
Embsay, $1\frac{1}{2}$ miles north-east of Skipton, access from A59.
Tel: (0756) 4727
Short length of track and good collection of steam locomotives. Steam trains run on Sundays and Bank holidays, Easter to September, plus Tuesdays in July and August. Also a number of special events.

SHOW CAVES

Opening times tend to vary and often depend on the weather or the number of visitors.

Ingleborough Cave
1½ miles north of Clapham, approached by footpath through Clapdale woods.
Tel: Clapham 242
Open: March to October November, daily; and February, daily (except Monday and Friday); December and January, Thursday, Saturday and Sunday.

Mother Shipton's Cave
Knaresborough.
Tel: (0423) 862352
On south bank of river approached from B6163. Reputed home of the fifteenth-century witch who prophesied many modern inventions.
Open most of the year.

Stump Cross Caverns
On B6265, Pateley Bridge to Grassington road, 5 miles west of Pateley Bridge. Easy access from road.
Tel: (0423) 752780
Fine stalactite and stalagmite formations. Visitor centre, café and gift shop.

White Scar Caves
1¾ miles north-east of Ingleton on B6255.
Tel: Ingleton 41244
Access from road. Ample car parking.
Open: February to November, daily, weather permitting.

Gaping Gill
3 miles north of Clapham, GR 751727.
Local caving club society organise winch descents, Spring and August Bank holidays.

BUS SERVICES

West Yorkshire Road Car Company
Tel: Skipton 5331

United Automobile Services Limited
Tel: Ripon 2093

Pennine
Tel: Gargrave 215

D. Whaites
12, High Hill Grove, Settle
Tel: Settle 3235

SHOW SPORTS AND EVENTS

Allendale New Year's Eve Fire Ceremony, New Year's Eve
Heptonstall Easter Pace Egg Play, Easter
Three Peaks Race, April
Gaping Gill Winch Descents, Bank holidays
Hardraw Band Contest, May
'Fellsmans' Hike from Ingleton, May
Farm Open Days (check with National Park leaflet)
Arkengarthdale Sports and Sheep Show, May
Street Market, Austwick, May
Wensleydale Horse Show, May
Tan Hill Sheep Show, May
Penyghent Race and Gala, Horton-in-Ribblesdale, June
Grassington Festival, June
Appleby Horse Fair, June
Hawes Sports (Horses and Sulkies), June
Bainbridge Sports (motorbikes), June
Hawes Gala, June
Malham Show, August
Reeth Show, August
Wensleydale Agricultural Show, August
Burnsall Sports, August
Hebden Sports, August
Upper Wharfedale Agricultural Show, Kilnsey, September
Swaledale Agricultural Show, Muker, September
Horton Show, September
Moorcock Show, Lunds, September
Redmire Feast, September
Nidderdale Agricultural Show, Pateley Bridge, September
Three Peaks Cycle Cross, September
The exact dates vary each year and details should be checked with information centres.

A weekly listing of activities taking place in Craven and around the Dales is published in the Craven News every Thursday under the heading 'Diary Dates'.

Autumn shows take place at Wolsingham, Egglestone and Stanhope.

MARKET DAYS

Appleby, Saturday (cattle: Monday, Friday)
Clitheroe, Tuesday, Saturday (cattle: Monday, Tuesday, Friday)
Barnard Castle, Wednesday
Gisburn, (cattle: Tuesday, Thursday)
Hawes, Tuesday
Ingleton, Friday
Kirkby Stephen, Monday
Kirkby Lonsdale, Thursday
Leyburn, Friday
Knaresborough, Wednesday (cattle: Thursday)
Middleton-in-Teesdale, Tuesday
Richmond, Saturday
Ripon, Thursday
Sedbergh, Wednesday (cattle: Friday)
Settle, Thursday
Skipton, Monday, Wednesday, Friday

YORKSHIRE DALES NATIONAL PARK

Colvend,
Hebdon Road
Grassington,
Skipton,
North Yorks B23 5LB
Tel: Grassington 752748

Whernside,
National Park Outdoor Recreation and Study Centre,
Dent,
Sedbergh,
Cumbria,
Tel: (05875) 213

Yorebridge House,
Bainbridge,
Leyburn,
North Yorks DL8 3BP
Tel: Wensleydale 50456

National Park Information Centres

Aysgarth Falls
    Tel: Aysgarth (09693) 424
Clapham,
    Tel: Clapham (04685) 419

Grassington, Hebden Bridge,
    Tel: Grassington (0756) 752748
Hawes, Station Road,
    Tel: Hawes (09697) 450
Malham,
    Tel: Airton (07293) 363
Sedbergh, Main Street,
    Tel: Sedbergh (0587) 20125

TOURIST INFORMATION CENTRES

Askrigg, Market Place,
    Tel: Wensleydale 50441
Barnard Castle, 43 Galgate,
    Tel: (0833) 38481 (weekdays)
    (0833) 37913 (Sundays/Saturdays)
Bentham, Station Road,
    Tel: Bentham 61043
Burnsall, Car Park Kiosk,
    Tel: Burnsall 295
Harrogate, Royal Baths Assembly Rooms,
    Crescent Road,
    Tel: (0423) 65912
Horton in Ribblesdale,
    Tel: Horton 333
Ingleton, Community Centre Car Park,
    Tel: Ingleton 41049
Ilkley,
    Tel: Ilkley 602319
Kirkby Lonsdale,
    Tel: Kirkby Lonsdale 71603
Leyburn, Central Garage, Market Place,
    Tel: Wensleydale 84373
Pateley Bridge,
    Tel: Harrogate 711147
Reeth, Swaledale Folk Museum, The Green
    Tel: Richmond 84373
Richmond, Friary Gardens, Queens Road,
    Tel: Richmond 3525
Settle, Town Hall,
    Tel: Settle 3617
Skipton, Town Hall Car Park,
    Tel: Skipton 2809

Information is also available from the Yorkshire and Humberside Tourist Board, Northumbrian Tourist Board and North West Tourist Boards (see under Accommodation for addresses and telephone numbers).

Wherever you find accommodation in the Yorkshire Dales you will find a warm welcome and a hospitality which is known throughout the world. In 1981 the first ever comprehensive Accommodation Guide was published by the Yorkshire Dales National Park Committee in conjunction with the Yorkshire Dales Tourist Association; look out for the white and brown cover.

Youth Hostels

There are youth hostels at,
Aysgarth Falls

Aysgarth,
Leyburn,
North Yorkshire
Tel: (09693) 260

Dacre Banks

The Old School,
Dacre Banks,
Harrogate,
North Yorkshire
Tel: (0423) 780431

Dentdale

Cowgill,
Dent,
Sedbergh,
Cumbria
Tel: (05875) 251

Earby,

Glen Cottage,
Birch Hall Lane,
Earby,
Colne,
Lancashire
Tel: (0282) 842349

Ellingstring

Lilac Cottage,
Ellingstring,
Ripon,
North Yorkshire

Enquiries to Yorkshire Region,
96 Main Street,
Bingley.

Grinton Lodge

Grinton,
Richmond,
North Yorkshire
Tel: (0748) 84206

Hawes,

Lancaster Terrace,
Hawes,
North Yorkshire
Tel: (09697) 368

Haworth

Longlands Hall,
Longlands Drive,
Lees Lane,
Haworth,
Keighley,
West Yorkshire
Tel: (0535) 42234

Ingleton

Greta Tower,
Ingleton,
Carnforth,
Lancashire
Tel: (0468) 41444

Keld,

Keld Lodge,
Richmond,
North Yorkshire
Tel: (0748) 86259

Kettlewell,

Whernside House,
Kettlewell,
Skipton,
North Yorkshire
Tel: (075676) 232

Linton,

The Old Rectory,
Linton-in-Craven,

Skipton,
North Yorkshire
Tel: (0756) 752400

Malham,

Malham
Skipton,
North Yorkshire
Tel: (07293) 321

Mankinholes Hall,

Mankinholes,
Todmorden,
Lancashire
Tel: (070681) 2340

Slaidburn,

King's House,
Slaidburn,
Clitheroe,
Lancashire
Tel: (02006) 656

Stainforth,

Stainforth,
Settle,
North Yorkshire
Tel: (07292) 3577

Some Tourist Information Centres, such as Settle, operate a 'Book-a-Bed' service. For a small fee they will find you the right sort of accommodation.
Information on accommodation outside the Yorkshire Dales National Park is obtainable from Tourist Boards as listed below:

Northumbria Tourist Board,
9 Osborne Terrace,
Jesmond,
Newcastle upon Tyne NE2 1NT
Tel: (0632) 817744

Yorkshire and Humberside Tourist Board,
312 Tadcaster Road,
York YO2 2HF
Tel: (0904) 707961

North West Tourist Board,
The Last Drop Village,

Bromley Cross,
Bolton,
Lancashire BL7 9PZ
Tel: (0204) 591511

ORGANISED HOLIDAYS AND COURSES

Yorkshire Dales Adventure Centre Trust Ltd,
Gildersleets,
Giggleswick,
Settle
Tel: (0792 92) 5359

HF Holidays Ltd.,
142 Great North Way,
London NW4 1EG
Tel: (01 203) 3381

Field Studies Council,
Malham Tarn Field Centre,
Settle,
North Yorkshire BD24 9PU
Tel: (072 93) 331

Birdguide,
Ashville,
Rose Bank,
Burley in Wharfedale,
West Yorkshire LS29 7PQ

The Dales Centre,
Grassington
Tel: (0756) 752757

Ramblers Holidays Ltd,
Box 43,
Welwyn Garden City,
Herts AL8 6PQ
Tel: Welwyn Garden (0707) 331133

Whernside Cave and Fell Centre,
Dent,
Sedbergh,
Cumbria
Tel: (05875) 213

YHA Adventure Holidays,
14 Southampton Street,
London WC2E 7HY

British Mountaineering Council,
Crawford House,
Precinct Centre,
Booth Street East,
Manchester M13 9RZ
Tel: (061 273) 5835

British Tourist Authority,
Information Centre,
Lower Regent Street,
London W1

Camping and Caravanning Club,
11 Lower Grosvenor Place,
London SW1W 0EY
Tel: (01 828) 1012

Caravan Club,
East Grinstead House,
East Grinstead,
Sussex RH19 1UA
Tel: (0342) 26944

Cyclists Touring Club,
69 Meadrow,
Godalming,
Surrey GU7 3HS
Tel: Godalming 7217

English Heritage,
Historic Buildings and Monuments
Commission for England,
23 Savile Row,
London W1X 2HE
Tel: (01 734) 6010

English Heritage,
North Office,
Arnhem Block,
Carlisle Castle,
Carlisle CA3 8UR
Tel: (0228) 31777

HF Holidays Ltd.,
142 Great North Way,
London NW4 1EG
Tel: (01 203) 3381

National Caving Association,
Whernside Cave and Fell Centre,
Yorkshire Dales National Park,
Dent,
Sedbergh,
Cumbria LA10 5RE
Tel: (05875) 213

National Trust,
36 Queen Anne's Gate,
London SW1H 9AS
Tel: (01 222) 9251

Outward Bound Trust,
Chestnut Field,
Regent Place,
Rugby CV21 2TJ
Tel: (0788) 60423/4/5

Ramblers' Association,
1-5 Wandsworth Road,
London SW8 2XX
Tel: (01 582) 6878

Yorkshire Wildlife Trust,
20 Castlegate,
York YO1 1RP
Tel: (0904) 59570

Youth Hostels Association,
Trevelyan House,
St Albans,
Herts AL1 2DY
Tel: (0727) 55215

YHA Yorkshire Regional Office,
96 Main Street,
Bingley,
West Yorkshire BD16 2JH
Tel: (0274) 567697

Bibliography

Bonser, K.J. The Drovers,
(Macmillan, 1970)
Calderdale Way Association,
The Calderdale Way, (1978)
Cowley, W. Farming in Yorkshire,
(Dalesman, 1972)
Duerden, N. Portrait of the Dales,
(Hale, 1978)
Hartley, M. and Ingilby, J.
The Yorkshire Dales
Life and Tradition in the Yorkshire
Dales
Hoole, K. Railways in the Yorkshire
Dales, (Dalesman, 1975)
Hoskins, W.G. English Landscapes,
(BBC, 1973)
Lousley, J.E. Wild Flowers of the Chalk
and Limestone, (Collins, 1950)
Mitchell, W.R. Wild Pennines,
(Hale, 1976)
Mitchell, W.R. & Joy, D. Settle-Carlisle
Railway, (Dalesman, 1969)
Mitchell, W.R. Pennine Birds,
(Dalesman, 1973)
Poucher, W.A. The Peak and the
Pennines, (Constable, 1966)
Raistrick, A. Green Roads in the Mid-
Pennines, (Moorland Publishing, 1978)
Old Yorkshire Dales, (David &
Charles, 1967)
The Pennine Dales, (Eyre &
Spottiswoode, 1968)
Malham and Malham Moor,
(Dalesman, 1971)
The Pennine Walls, (Dalesman, 1973)
Lead Mining in the Mid-Pennines,
(Bradford Barton 1973)
The Lead Industry of Wensleydale and
Swaledale:
Vol I The Mines, (Moorland
Publishing, 1974)

The Lead Industry of Wensleydale and
Swaledale:
Vol II The Smelting Mills,
(Moorland Publishing, 1975)
Raistrick, A. Buildings in the Yorkshire
Dales, (Dalesman, 1976)
Simmons, E.G.(Ed), Yorkshire Dales
National Park, (HMSO, 1971)
Speakman, C. Transport in Yorkshire,
(Dalesman, 1969)
The Dales Way, (Dalesman 1970)
A Yorkshire Dales Anthology,
(Hale, 1981)
Stephenson, T. The Pennine Way,
(HMSO, 1969)
Wainwright, A. Pennine Way
Companion, (Westmorland Gazette,
1969)
Walks on the Howgill Fells,
(Westmorland Gazette, 1968)
Walks in Limestone Country,
(Westmorland Gazette, 1968)
Wood, G. Bernard, Yorkshire Villages,
(Hale, 1971)
Yorkshire Dales National Park Plan,
(Yorkshire Dales National Park,
1976)
Wright, G.N. The Yorkshire Dales,
(David & Charles, 1977)
View of Northumbria, (Hale, 1981)
Roads and Trackways of the
Yorkshire Dales, (Moorland, 1985)

Some of these books are out of print. Your
local library should, however, be able to
obtain a copy.

Index

THE VISITOR'S GUIDE SERIES

- ☐ The Black Forest
- ☐ Brittany
- ☐ Chilterns
- ☐ Cornwall and Isles of Scilly
- ☐ Cotswolds
- ☐ Devon
- ☐ Dordogne
- ☐ East Anglia
- ☐ The French Coast
- ☐ Florence & Tuscany
- ☐ Guernsey Alderney and Sark
- ☐ Hampshire & The Isle of Wight
- ☐ Historic Places of Wales
- ☐ Iceland
- ☐ Kent
- ☐ Lake District
- ☐ Loire
- ☐ Normandy
- ☐ North Wales and Snowdonia
- ☐ North York Moors, York & Yorkshire Coast
- ☐ Peak District (revised edition)
- ☐ Severn & Avon
- ☐ Scottish Borders & Edinburgh
- ☐ Somerset & Dorset
- ☐ South & West Wales
- ☐ South of France
- ☐ Sussex
- ☐ Tyrol
- ☐ Welsh Borders
- ☐ Yorkshire Dales, Teesdale & Weardale

also

- ☐ Walking in the Alps
- ☐ Walking in Switzerland

If you have enjoyed this Visitor's Guide from Moorland,

why not look at some of our other county and country-wide books?

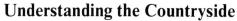

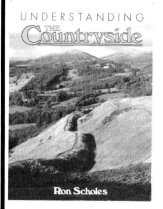

Understanding the Countryside

A study of man's impact on the landscape and the remains he left: how to recognise significant features and where to go to find them. *(Hardback)*

Byways of Britain

100 out-of-the-way places in ten different areas (including the Yorkshire Dales and the North York Moors), with suggested walks and places of interest away from the crowds. *(Hardback)*

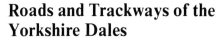

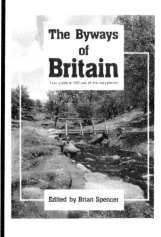

Roads and Trackways of the Yorkshire Dales

Yorkshire has a network of old roads and tracks which criss-cross its countryside. These ways have an intriguing history, and this book examines how they came into being. Of great interest to both historian and country lover. *(Hardback)*

Visitor's Guide to the North York Moors, York and the Yorkshire Coast

A companion to the Yorkshire Dales guide, covering the remainder of Yorkshire.